W9-BWJ-617

The Organization of

Mental Abilities

IN THE AGE RANGE 13 TO 17

JEROME EDWARD DOPPELT, Ph.D.

TEACHERS COLLEGE, COLUMBIA UNIVERSITY
CONTRIBUTIONS TO EDUCATION, NO. 962

BUREAU OF PUBLICATIONS

TEACHERS COLLEGE · COLUMBIA UNIVERSITY

NEW YORK · 1950

Library of Congress Cataloging in Publication Data

Doppelt, Jerome Edward.
   The organization of mental abilities in the age range
13 to 17.

   Reprint of the 1950 ed., issued in series: Teachers
College, Columbia University. Contributions to educa-
tion, no. 962.
   Originally presented as the author's thesis, Columbia.
   Bibliography: p.
   1. Ability--Testing. 2. Adolescence. I. Title.
II. Series: Columbia University. Teachers College.
Contributions to education, no. 962.
BF431.D65 1972   153.9'4   71-176725
ISBN 0-404-55962-X

From the edition of 1950, New York
First AMS edition published in 1972
Manufactured in the United States

AMS PRESS, INC.
NEW YORK, N. Y.   10003

ACKNOWLEDGMENTS

I welcome the opportunity to express my gratitude to Professor Irving Lorge, sponsor of this study, for his guidance and aid, and to Professors Robert L. Thorndike and Helen M. Walker for their invaluable suggestions and criticisms.

I am also deeply indebted to Drs. G. K. Bennett, H. G. Seashore, and A. G. Wesman, authors of the Differential Aptitude Tests, and to The Psychological Corporation, publisher of the tests, for making available to me the vast amount of data gathered in the standardization program for the test battery.

J. E. D.

CONTENTS

TABLES

The Organization of Mental Abilities

IN THE AGE RANGE 13 TO 17

1

INTRODUCTION

DURING the past two decades there has been considerable development in the field of mental measurement. The tendency has been to move away from a single over-all measure of a subject's "ability" to measurement of components of ability. For guidance work it has been found much more useful to have knowledge of an individual's standing in each of several different abilities than to have only a single estimate of his "intelligence." Closely associated with the development of tests for various abilities is the increase in the study of interrelationships among abilities. As more tests are developed for measuring the abilities of groups of individuals, more data are potentially available for the study of interrelationships under different conditions. It becomes possible to investigate the organization pattern of selected abilities and to note the effects on organization of such variables as age, sex, and the selection of cases.

At one time it was generally assumed that the interrelationships among abilities remained more or less constant. Asch [3],* writing in 1936, noted: "In spite of the enormous amount of evidence concerning the changes which continually occur in behavior, stu-

* Numbers in brackets refer to bibliographical references, pages 83–84.

1

dents of mental organization have assumed, almost without exception, that the *relationships* between mental performances remain constant during the life of the individual, and that changes accompanying growth and learning leave these relationships unchanged." Asch went on to question this assumption of the constancy of mental organization. There has since been put forth the general idea that changes in mental organization do occur with growth of the individual. Garrett [12] has elaborated a very interesting hypothesis, based on experimental studies, which he states as follows: "Abstract or symbol intelligence changes in its organization as age increases from a fairly unified and general ability to a loosely organized group of abilities or factors. . . . From these various studies I believe we can predict a steady drop in correlation among tests involving verbal, numerical and spatial concepts from about age 8 to age 18. With increasing age there appears to be a gradual breakdown of an amorphous general ability into a group of fairly distinct aptitudes."

The phenomenon of change in mental organization has by now received more general acceptance. However, it must not be assumed that such change is inevitable—that it will occur at all age levels and in all abilities. It is possible, for example, that under certain conditions a general ability factor may remain relatively invariant. The key words in this statement of possibility are "under certain conditions," a phrase which conveniently covers the problems of test instruments, selection of subjects, and precise definition of terms. These problems are continuously present in any study, and the ways in which they are treated materially influence the results.

Recognizing, then, the importance of "certain conditions," the present study is proposed to test the hypothesis that there is a reduction in the amount of undifferentiated general ability, or, conversely, an increase in the specialization of ability components, as age increases.

2

RELATED STUDIES

A SURVEY of the literature discloses that information with regard to the problem of the relationship of age to mental organization may be obtained in two general ways. In brief, these two ways may be categorized as (1) selection from independent studies of different age groups evidence which relates to the problem and (2) examination of studies which were aimed directly at the problem of age and mental organization.

The first category includes studies which did not have as their primary purpose the direct comparison of the mental organization of different age groups. Each of them, however, has made some contribution to knowledge of the organization pattern of a particular age group, and the findings for different groups may be compared. The second category includes investigations in which different age groups were studied as part of the original experimental design. Some of these studies used the same subjects before and after an interval of time and drew conclusions with regard to the mental organization of the subjects at different ages. Other studies in the second category dealt simultaneously with subjects representative of different ages.

COMPARISONS OF INDEPENDENT STUDIES

Independent studies of specific age groups are relevant to the problem of the present study only insofar as the findings for different age levels may be compared. Ideally, one study would show the relationship between abilities X and Y for one age level while another study would show the relationship between the *same* abilities for a second age level. Such identity of the variables is, of course, impossible with studies which had different purposes and used different materials. Another point which must be considered when comparing results for different groups is the effect of selection of cases. It is virtually impossible to guarantee the same degree of selectivity for the two or more groups compared. In the circumstances, the only possible procedure is to compare findings with regard to similar or related aspects of mental organization, while keeping in mind that the variables are not identical even when their names are the same and that differential factors of selection may influence the results. Among the independent studies, the findings of the following pairs (listed by authors) may be compared: Thorndike and Garrett, Bryan and Anastasi, Schiller and Schneck, and L. L. and T. G. Thurstone.

Thorndike [23] reported a correlation coefficient of .52 between vocabulary and arithmetic on the CAVD Intelligence Scale for 126 pupils in grade 5.5. He also reported a correlation of .23 between vocabulary and arithmetical problems for 100 university students. In a footnote, however, he makes the following comment: "The arithmetical tasks were not hard enough to measure the ability of the group well, and the correlations would probably be considerably higher with an adequate set of mathematical tasks." Garrett [10] confirmed the lower correlation for the older group in a study based on 313 college freshman women. He found a correlation coefficient of .21 between vocabulary and arithmetic on the CAVD.

Bryan [6], in her work with 200 children between the ages of 5 and 6, found that various tests of memory were as closely related to tests of general intelligence and verbal ability as they were to each other. She had given eleven tests of memory for various types of material, a vocabulary test, and the Stanford-Binet Test of Intelligence. The average intercorrelations among the eleven memory tests were .38 for boys and .31 for girls; the average correlations of vocabulary and the Stanford-Binet with the memory tests were, respectively, .45 and .49 for boys and .35 and .41 for girls. The memory tests were selected to measure the ability to retain impressions while avoiding the introduction of special abilities. The criterion for the selection of the tests was that they should differ with respect to material, form, modality of presentation, mode of response, degree of complexity, and interval of delay.

Anastasi's [1] work with college students, however, indicated that immediate memory for various types of material bore little, if any, relationship to vocabulary, arithmetic reasoning, or spatial ability. She tested a group of 225 men students from the College of the City of New York and found an average correlation coefficient of .06 between her battery of eight immediate memory tests and vocabulary, .15 between memory and arithmetic reasoning, and .14 between memory and spatial ability (Minnesota Paper Form Board Test). The average intercorrelation coefficient of the memory tests was .40. (These are coefficients corrected for attenuation.) In a later study with 140 women college students, Anastasi [2] concluded that the results "fully corroborate the former results on the memory, verbal and numerical factors, and their mutual independence."

Schiller [18], studying the problem of mental organization among school children, administered twelve tests to 189 boys and 206 girls whose average age was 9 years. Of the twelve tests, four were classified as verbal, three as numerical, and five as spatial-manipulation tests. The average correlation coefficients between the verbal and number tests were .62 for boys and .60 for girls; between the verbal and spatial tests they were .38 for boys and .46 for girls; between number and spatial tests they were .40 for boys and .46 for girls. A factor analysis by Garrett [11] of Schiller's data for boys showed a correlation coefficient of .83 between the verbal and number factors.

On the other hand, Schneck [19], in a study based on 210 college men, reported a correlation coefficient of .26 between his factors of verbal ability and numerical ability. He had given five verbal and four numerical tests and identified two factors as "general factors for verbal ability and for numerical ability."

Factorial studies made by L. L. and T. G. Thurstone [24,26] based on groups at different age levels showed that the primary factors which were extracted were more closely related for eighth-grade children than they were for subjects ranging in age from 16 to 25. The relationship among the factors for the younger group was taken as evidence of a "second-order general factor," probably equivalent to Spearman's g, which was not found with the older group.

An examination of these studies seems to justify the hypothesis that differentiation among abilities is greater for the older age groups than it is for the younger. This hypothesis may be entirely valid. However, it must be noted that there is an important reservation to be placed on it. The studies which have been compared, although they may have used similar materials (tests), did not use the *same* materials with the different age levels. Correlation techniques are methods for comparing the order of individuals on the basis of one variable with their order on the basis of a second variable. As one or both of the variables change, the correlation coefficient changes. When coefficients based on different pairs of tests are compared, there are a number of additional sources of variation that may influence the size and reliability of the difference between the coefficients: differences in content and form of the tests, differences in reliability and validity of the tests, and differences in the administration and scoring of the tests, as well as differences in the degree of selectivity of the groups. The limitation inherent in the use of different materials is present in any comparison of the results of one study with those of another study based on different variables. This point is also emphasized by Schiller [18]: "The fact that two tests present the same type of task to the subject does not mean that those tests measure the identical ability. A vocabulary test devised for 9-year-old children by one experimenter does not necessarily tap the same ability as a vocabulary test devised for 12-year-old children. To be fairly certain that the same ability is being measured in both groups, a single test must be devised adequate to test both the dullest 9-year-old and the brightest 12-year-old. Correlations and pattern analyses would then have a more consistent meaning from group to group."

STUDIES DIRECTLY CONCERNED WITH THE PROBLEM

Investigators of the specific problem of the relationship of age to mental organization have, in general, used the same tests with different age groups. Two approaches have been taken in the selection of subjects for studies. Some investigators have tested the same cases before and after an interval of time. One such study was made by Asch [3] in 1936. Asch gave 79 boys and 82 girls, first at age 9 and again at age 12, four verbal tests and three numerical tests. His results showed a marked decrease in correlations between ages 9 and 12, and he found a restriction in the size of the factor of "general ability" between those ages. Unfortunately, however, the tests were not identical for the two testings. "It was necessary to increase all the power tests in difficulty at the second testing to correspond with the increased mental level of the subjects. This was done by the addition of more difficult items to the tests earlier administered."

Another study in which the same subjects and the same tests were used before and after an interval of time is reported by Swineford [21]. Six tests were administered twice to two groups of pupils, 212 in grades 8 and 9 and 173 in grades 7 and 9. The tests, taking about two hours of testing time, included three "which measure the general intellective bi-factor (arithmetic, series completion, and deduction) and three which measure both the general and the verbal bi-factors (general information, reading comprehension, and word meaning)." Swineford reports small but statistically significant practice effects in four of the tests after the one-year interval and in one of the first three tests (series completion) after the two-year interval. Her other findings are summarized thus:

"A most significant finding is that the factor composition of the six tests does not change materially during the two years represented by the data. The general factor identified by the tests administered in grade 7 can be interpreted as the same factor as that identified by the same tests administered one or two years later.

"No evidence is found to support the view that with increasing mental maturity the general factor plays a less important role as special abilities are developed. On the contrary, the general ability represented in the present data increases in both its absolute and its relative contribution to the total test variance."

A second approach within the general framework of using the same tests has been to select different age groups and to test them simultaneously. Comparisons are then made among the successive age groups. A fundamental study using this approach is the one by Garrett, Bryan, and Perl [13] in 1935. These authors worked with age levels 9–10, 12–13, and 15–16. The tests used were six memory tests and four non-memory tests—a motor speed test, a vocabulary

test, an arithmetic test, and a revision of the Minnesota Paper
Form Board. The study was made separately for boys and girls and
the authors tried to avoid special selection in their groups. They
report a "fairly consistent tendency for the average r's to decrease
with age." They also did a Thurstone multiple factor analysis for
each age and sex group and found one large factor which was interpreted as "general ability to perform mental tasks of the kind
presented by our tests." It was reported that "the first factor accounts for progressively less of the variance of the ten tests (except
at age 12, boys) as age increases," and the conclusion was that
"between 9 and 15 abilities of the sort here measured become more
specific with age." The study by Garrett, Bryan, and Perl is one
of the important early investigations of the problem of age and
mental organization. It will be reviewed in greater detail in a subsequent chapter. It should be noted at this point, however, that
it is doubtful whether the results obtained permit definite, clear-
cut conclusions. For example, the average intercorrelations at ages
9, 12, and 15 were .30, .21, and .18 for boys, and .27, .30, and .10
for girls. It is difficult to evaluate the significance of the difference
between ages 12 and 15 for the boys, and in the case of the girls
there is an actual rise from age 9 to age 12. The results of the
several factor analyses made by Garrett, Bryan, and Perl will be
discussed later.

In 1944 Clark [7] investigated the problem of changes in mental
organization with respect to certain defined abilities at three stages
in the growth curve. She used the Chicago Test of Primary Mental
Abilities, which yields scores on six primary mental abilities or
components—Number, Verbal Meaning, Space, Word Fluency,
Reasoning, and Memory. The subjects were 11-, 13-, and 15-year-
old boys in New York City public schools. A very interesting aspect of this study was that the age groups were roughly equated
for general intelligence as determined by group test IQ scores.
Clark reports a consistent decrease in the intercorrelations among
the six abilities, except for the memory factor, as age increased.
She also found that "with the exception of the memory component, changes with age in the primary mental abilities were not
noticeably influenced by the general intelligence level of the subjects as indicated by intelligence tests."

Reichard [17] tried to utilize an experimental setup in which all variables other than age were carefully controlled. Her subjects were 9-, 12-, and 15-year-old children. The tests were constructed for the study to measure each of four factors: verbal, number, memory, and spatial ability. The final battery consisted of eight tests—three of verbal ability, two of number ability, two of memory ability, and one of spatial ability. The average correlations among the eight tests showed an increase from ages 9 to 12 and a decrease from ages 12 to 15. Reichard also made a multiple factor analysis of her data, computing only the first factor loadings. The first factor, identified as a general factor, accounted for an increasing amount of the variance between the ages of 9 and 12 and for a decreasing amount between the ages of 12 and 15. She concluded that there is a gradual increase in integration of mental ability which reaches a maximum at approximately 12 years of age, after which there is a decrease in relationship due to the crystallizing out of group factors.

In 1946, Blumenfeld [5] reported a study in which he had examined some 650 male children of the Lima, Peru, primary and secondary schools with an adaptation of the Terman Group Test of Mental Ability for Grades 7–12. The subjects were in the fourth and fifth grades of the primary school and in the first and second grades of the secondary school with ages ranging from 12 to 16 years. He investigated the correlations among six of the possible pairs of subtests of the Terman test for each age group from 12 to 16. There was no distinct trend as age increased. Intertest correlations for the groups arranged according to school grade gave the same result, although in this case there existed a clear progress in the mean scores. This conclusion was tentatively put forth by Blumenfeld: "As far as test performances are concerned, the coefficients of correlation which we have found seem to depend rather exclusively upon the nature of the tests and not upon the age of the subjects and their level of maturation."

A monograph recently published by Swineford [22] confirms some of the conclusions of an earlier study by the same author [21] and has important implications for the present investigation. Swineford used the bi-factor method of factor analysis to investigate the nature of the three bi-factors—general, verbal, and spatial.

Her data consisted of scores on nine tests (Arithmetic, Series Completion, Deduction, General Information, Reading Comprehension, Word Meaning, Punched Holes, Drawings, and Visual Imagery) administered to 952 pupils in grades 5–10 inclusive. The conclusions with regard to the general factor are of particular interest: "The patterns for the six grade groups show fluctuations in pattern weights from one grade to the next but no systematic change. There is no indication whatever that the general factor tends to disappear with increasing mental maturity as suggested by Wright, during the period covered by Grades V–X. That is, not only is the factor measured by all the tests at all levels but also the correlations of factor with tests tend to be similar for all grade groups."

SUMMARY

If, at this point, the implications of the various studies cited are to be considered, a number of summarizing statements may be made. The studies made by independent investigators, which were considered in pairs in the foregoing discussion, suggest that the extent of relationship between test variables and, in some instances, between factors, decreases with increasing age. This conclusion, however, is seriously limited by the fact that the measuring instruments are not the same from study to study. This, of course, is not a fault of the original studies, which were not aimed at the problem of comparing the mental organization of different age groups. But it is a limitation when inferences are made on the basis of those studies with reference to the problem now being considered.

The second group of studies cited did use the identical tests with various age groups and do not suffer from the weakness of different measuring instruments. (An exception to this is the study by Asch, where the tests were changed somewhat for the second testing.) Here, however, there is a lack of uniformity among the conclusions from the various studies. Garrett, Bryan, and Perl present evidence for increasing differentiation and decreasing importance of a general factor as age increases. Swineford presents data which show no decrease in a general factor as age increases. The studies by Asch and by Clark more or less support the findings of Garrett,

Bryan, and Perl. Reichard's study in part supports the same findings and in part contradicts them. Asch and Reichard do not agree for ages 9 and 12. Blumenfeld, in his study, reported no evidence of change in correlation coefficients as age increased from 12 to 16, and thus seems to come closest to Swineford.

A further complication which must be considered in dealing with different age groups is the possibility of some type of selection of subjects in the older groups. This is especially true when the subjects are school children. Older groups are at a higher educational level and tend to be somewhat more homogeneous with respect to ability than younger groups. There are times when the selection process is not very obvious, but the net result is the same whether selection is obvious or subtle: the variability of the older groups is reduced. With smaller variability, correlation coefficients also tend to be reduced. When the extent of correlation between variables decreases as age increases, it is important to determine whether or not a selection factor is responsible for the decrease in relationship.

If the problem is to determine a definite, unequivocal answer to the effect of age on mental organization, then it would appear that no such answer is possible. It becomes apparent that the problem is too complex for a simple solution. The materials used in the investigation, the age groups considered, and the methods of analysis all tend to influence the results. Each study can explore only a limited phase of the problem and contribute its share to a greater understanding of the total situation. One of the promising approaches is to investigate the change in the so-called "general factor." This is the convenient name for whatever it is that runs through all abilities. It has been variously associated with general intelligence, general ability, power, and what Spearman has called g. In factorial studies it is the factor which shows high correlation with all the tests. If a factor could reasonably be identified as a "general ability" factor than it should be profitable to determine whether it progressively increases or decreases in importance as age increases. Does the relationship between tests and general ability change as age increases? Such investigations may contribute valuable information toward a better understanding of the relationship between age and mental organization.

Garrett, Bryan, and Perl made factor analyses of their various age groups and identified a general factor which they then proceeded to study. Swineford, Asch, and Reichard also worked with a general factor. But one thing that becomes clear from examination of these and other factorial studies is that a "general factor" does not always mean the same thing. It depends on the materials from which it has been extracted. If, for example, all the tests used in a hypothetical study were tests of memory, then the general factor would be some kind of general memory factor. Further, one set of memory tests may not yield the same memory factor as a second set. In summarizing a series of her studies, Anastasi [2] concluded that "we cannot speak of a single common factor running through *all* forms of memory." If all the tests were of numerical ability, then there would probably be something akin to a general number factor extracted. In addition to having several kinds of general factors, it is also entirely possible, theoretically, to get a general factor with one age group which may be different from the general factor of another age group. Comparisons that are then made from group to group would suffer from a certain amount of ambiguity.

This study proposed to extract a general ability factor from a battery of tests constructed to serve the functions of guidance. The general factor should then be closely allied to the kind of general ability that runs through a number of significant and distinct areas of knowledge. It was further proposed to make the analysis in a way that definitely establishes the identity of the general factor from age level to age level.

With a general factor carefully defined, and with comparisons based on the same variables, it is hoped that the study will contribute a little to a solution of the problem of mental organization at the age levels considered.

3

THE PROBLEM AND PROCEDURE

THE BASIC problem of this study may be put rather simply as a question: Does the general factor decrease in importance as age increases? But, as has been indicated earlier, the definition of terms and conditions of the experiment are important determiners of the results. It is therefore advisable to define, as early as possible, the term "general factor" and to indicate the framework within which the study was conducted.

The general factor is thought of in this study as the underlying common core of a number of different abilities. As such it ought to be general in the sense of being general power or general reasoning ability or general intelligence. If measures of highly related abilities are investigated, it may be that the factor common to all of them is a general form of a particular kind of ability—general memory or a general mechanical ability factor, for example. Obviously, the abilities measured must have a certain amount of overlap or there would be no common factor. But the abilities should be quite distinct, so that what they share in common is most reasonably identified as general ability in the sense of general underlying power. It should be noted that a number of tests may be completely different from each other with regard to content but so similar in conditions of administration as to make speed an important aspect of each of them. To avoid possible contamination of the general factor by speed it was felt desirable to use, in so far as possible, a series of power tests.

The criteria for the selection of tests to be used were thus determined by the kind of general factor that was to be investigated. In order to obtain a common factor related as much as possible to general power, the tests from which it was to be extracted must be measures of different abilities from which the effects of speed are largely removed. It is, of course, impossible to eliminate completely the influence of speed from a test with definite time limits, but it is possible to reduce it considerably by allowing sufficient time for completion of the tests.

A battery of tests which seemed to satisfy the criteria set forth above is the series known as the Differential Aptitude Tests, published by The Psychological Corporation. The manual [8] of the battery states: "The purpose of the Differential Aptitude Tests is to provide an integrated, scientific, and well-standardized procedure for measuring the abilities of boys and girls in grades eight through twelve for purposes of educational and vocational guidance. . . . On the basis of these studies eight tests were selected for inclusion in the battery. These tests gave promise of providing *adequate reliability* of measurement in reasonable testing periods, of having sufficiently *low intercorrelations* to indicate they were measuring different aptitudes, and of being *valid predictors* for a large variety of educational curricula and vocational fields." These tests satisfied the criterion of measuring in different areas and had the further advantage of measuring in areas of real significance. That is to say, they measure in areas that are of importance in a practical sense and are thus more likely to encompass a true situation than tests specifically designed for a theoretical problem. With one exception (the Clerical Speed and Accuracy Test) the Differential Aptitude Tests are power tests with time limits such that most subjects are able to attempt all items. They therefore meet adequately the requirement that the effect of speed be kept to a minimum.

THE TESTS

A description of the eight tests and the time allowed for each is given below. Illustrative items from the various tests are shown on pages 16 and 17.

1. *Verbal Reasoning.*—The Verbal Reasoning test is intended as a measure of ability to understand concepts framed in words. It is aimed at the evaluation of the student's ability to abstract or generalize and to think constructively rather than of simple fluency or vocabulary recognition. The questions are in the form of

analogies that are open at both ends. The student is required to select two words out of eight possible options which will complete the analogy. Time: 30 minutes.

2. *Numerical Ability.*—The Numerical Ability test is designed to test understanding of numerical relationships and facility in handling numerical concepts. The problems are of the "arithmetic computation" type in order to avoid undue emphasis on reading ability. Some items test only for skill in numerical processes; others call for real understanding of numerical relationships. The manual reports: "It has been demonstrated by actual tryout in the schools that they (the problems) are sufficiently complex to challenge students in all high school grades." Time: 30 minutes.

3. *Abstract Reasoning.*—The Abstract Reasoning test is intended as a non-verbal measure of the student's reasoning ability. Each problem consists of a series of four diagrams and the student is required to discover the principle or principles governing the change of the figures. He gives evidence of his understanding by selecting out of five possible choices the diagram which should logically follow. The task in each problem may be characterized as thinking with abstract symbols. Time: 25 minutes.

4. *Space Relations.*—The Space Relations test requires mental manipulation of objects in three-dimensional space. The items are measures of the ability to visualize a constructed object from a picture of a pattern and also the ability to imagine how the object would appear if rotated in various ways. No premium is placed on visual discrimination. The task is concerned solely with judgments of how the objects would look if constructed and rotated. Time: 30 minutes.

5. *Mechanical Reasoning.*—The Mechanical Reasoning test is a series of items each of which consists of a pictorially presented mechanical situation together with a simply worded question. The items are presented in terms of simple, frequently encountered mechanisms that do not resemble textbook illustration. Time: 30 minutes.

6. *Clerical Speed and Accuracy.*—The Clerical Speed and Accuracy test is intended to measure speed of response in a simple perceptual task. The student must select the combination of numbers and letters which is marked in the test booklet, then bear it in

EXAMPLES OF ITEMS IN THE DIFFERENTIAL APTITUDE TESTS*
WITH SELECTED PORTIONS OF TEST DIRECTIONS

VERBAL REASONING

Each of the fifty sentences in this test has the first word and the last word left out. You are to pick out words which will fill the blanks so that the sentence will be true and sensible.

EXAMPLE Z. .....is to night as breakfast is to.....

1. flow	2. gentle	3. supper	4. door
A. include	B. morning	C. enjoy	D. corner

NUMERICAL ABILITY

This test consists of forty numerical problems. Next to each problem there are five answers. You are to pick out the correct answer and fill in the space under its letter on the separate Answer Sheet.

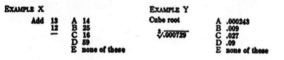

EXAMPLE X

Add 13
    12
    —

A 14
B 25
C 16
D 59
E none of these

EXAMPLE Y

Cube root

$\sqrt[3]{.000729}$

A .000243
B .009
C .027
D .09
E none of these

ABSTRACT REASONING

Each row consists of four figures called Problem Figures and five called Answer Figures. The four Problem Figures make a series. You are to find out which one of the Answer Figures would be the next, or the fifth one in the series.

EXAMPLE X

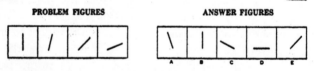

PROBLEM FIGURES   ANSWER FIGURES

SPACE RELATIONS

EXAMPLE X

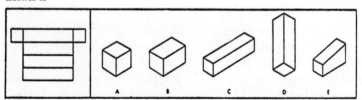

Which of these five figures — A, B, C, D, E — can be made from the pattern in Example X?

* Reproduced with the permission of The Psychological Corporation.

TEST EXAMPLES (*Continued*)

MECHANICAL REASONING

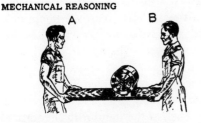

X

Which man has the heavier load?
(If equal, mark C.)

CLERICAL SPEED AND ACCURACY

You are to look at the one combination which is underlined, find the same one after that item number on the separate Answer Sheet, and fill in the space under it.

TEST ITEMS

V. <u>AB</u>	AC	AD	AE	AF
W. aA	aB	BA	Ba	<u>Bb</u>
X. A7	7A	B7	<u>7B</u>	AB
Y. Aa	Ba	<u>bA</u>	BA	bB
Z. 3A	3B	<u>33</u>	B3	BB

SAMPLE OF ANSWER SHEET

V	AC	AE	AF	AB	AD
W	BA	Ba	Bb	aA	aB
X	7B	B7	AB	7A	A7
Y	Aa	bA	bB	Ba	BA
Z	BB	3B	B3	3A	33

SPELLING

If the spelling of the word is right, fill in the space under RIGHT. If it is spelled wrong, fill in the space under WRONG.

EXAMPLES

W. man

X. allowence

SAMPLE OF ANSWER SHEET

	RIGHT	WRONG
W		
	RIGHT	WRONG
X		

SENTENCES

When you have decided which parts are wrong, fill in the space under those letters after that item number on the separate Answer Sheet.

EXAMPLE

Ain't we / going to the / office / next week / at all.
  A   B   C   D   E

SAMPLE OF ANSWER SHEET

A	B	C	D	E

The man who / everybody likes / is one / who / they can trust.
  A   B   C   D   E

mind while seeking the same combination in a group of similar combinations, and, having found the identical combination, he must underline it. Time: 6 minutes.

7. *Spelling.*—The Spelling test consists of 100 words selected from Gates's "Spelling Difficulties in 3876 Words." Some of the words are correctly spelled and others are incorrectly spelled. The student is to indicate, for each word, whether it is "right" or "wrong." Time: 10 minutes.

8. *Sentences.*—The Sentences test is intended to measure the student's ability to distinguish between good and bad grammar, punctuation, and word usage. Each of the items is in the form of a sentence marked off into five parts. The student must inspect each part of each sentence and judge whether or not it is correct. Time: 25 minutes.

The only speeded test in the battery is Clerical Speed and Accuracy. All the other tests allow enough time for most students to attempt all the items.

THE SUBJECTS

To investigate the problem of the relationship between mental organization and age it seems logical to use subjects who are below the age of adulthood. The phenomena of growth, both physical and mental, are most marked in the years of childhood and adolescence. If there is reorganization of abilities, it would probably be most evident during those years. It is not meant to imply that mental reorganization does not occur once adulthood has been reached. Actually, mental reorganization in adults is an important problem which needs considerable experimental investigation. But changes proceed at a much slower rate with adults than with children; an experiment with adult subjects would require groups that are spread relatively far apart in age in order to disclose differences, if any, in mental organization. It is, unfortunately, extremely difficult to obtain a sufficiently large number of cases, over a wide age range, and suitable measuring instruments for all of them. The problem is further complicated by the number of outside influences in the lives of adults which may affect the data. The difficulties inherent in the use of adults to investigate the problem of mental organization explain why most investigators have used young subjects. Garrett, Bryan, and Perl [13] worked with 9-, 12-, and 15-year-old children; Clark [7] with 11-, 13-, and 15-year-old boys; Reichard [17] with 9-, 12-, and 15-year-old children, and Asch [3] with 9- and 12-year-olds.

An interesting question, however, is raised: What happens if the upper limit of the age range studied is extended somewhat— perhaps to age 17 or 18? Is there much change between 14 and 18 or 13 and 18? There is the possibility that changes in mental organization may cease, more or less, at 13 or 14, and the pattern of organization remain constant for many years thereafter. The ages between 13 and 17 or 18 seem especially interesting to investigate, since during those years the rate of growth has slowed down considerably. In this period, moreover, educational and vocational guidance begin to assume increasingly important roles. A counselor may find it useful to know whether or not there is an increasing differentiation among abilities as the student goes through high school. Perhaps the differentiation is as marked at the beginning of high school as it is when the student graduates. Guidance given to high school students might be positively influenced by such information.

It thus seemed desirable to the writer to make the subjects in this study a group of children whose age range partially overlapped the ranges of earlier investigations and went some years beyond. This range, roughly from 13 to 18, represents an important developmental stage in children's lives; information as to the organization of abilities at this stage might be especially useful.

The data used in this study were collected in the elaborate standardization program for the Differential Aptitude Tests. These data included the test results of 21,994 students in grades 8 through 12 tested in thirty school systems in Northeastern and Midwestern states. From this reservoir of cases the students who had taken Form A of the battery were selected for study. These included students ranging in age from 12 to 19. However, the 12-year-old and the 18- and 19-year-old populations were not adequately represented by testing in grades 8 through 12. The age groups investigated were therefore restricted to those from 13 through 17, where the sampling was considerably more adequate with respect to grade representation.

RELIABILITY OF THE TESTS

Since the subjects of this study were taken directly from the standardization population for the test battery, there is available in the manual for the tests an indication of the reliability of each test. The reliability coefficients are given by grade and separately for each sex. Although the subjects in this study were classified primarily according to age, the correlation between age and grade placement is sufficiently high ($r = .85$ for boys; $r = .88$ for girls) to permit the acceptance of the reliability coefficients in the manual. Further evidence for the acceptability of the coefficients reported in the manual comes from a comparison of grade and age variability. The average standard deviations for the group reported in the manual (the average of the grade standard deviations) were compared with the average standard deviations computed by age for the experimental population. This comparison does not disclose any important changes in variability which might affect the size of the reliability coefficients when subjects are classified by age rather than grade. Table I presents the average standard deviations by grade and by age together with the grade reliability coefficients for each sex based on a sampling of the standardization population.

TABLE I*

AVERAGE STANDARD DEVIATIONS BY GRADE AND BY AGE AND MEAN RELIABILITY COEFFICIENTS OF THE DIFFERENTIAL APTITUDE TESTS BY SEX

TEST	AVERAGE GRADE S.D. (TEST MANUAL)		AVERAGE AGE S.D. (EXPERIMENTAL POPULATION)		RELIABILITY (MEAN r)	
	Boys	Girls	Boys	Girls	Boys	Girls
Verbal Reasoning	10.1	9.6	10.9	10.4	.90	.90
Numerical Ability	9.2	8.2	9.5	8.7	.90	.86
Abstract Reasoning	10.8	11.3	11.3	11.4	.90	.89
Space Relations	25.8	21.7	24.7	20.2	.93	.90
Mechanical Reasoning	13.2	10.4	13.1	10.5	.85	.71
Clerical Speed and Accuracy	11.8	12.5	12.6	13.5	.87	.87
Spelling	26.9	25.8	27.5	25.9	.92	.92
Sentences	16.6	16.5	17.5	17.4	.88	.87
N	960	1064	737	786	960	1064

* Adapted from Table II of the manual for the Differential Aptitude Tests [8].

The reliability coefficients are generally very high. When it is recalled that these coefficients were computed for groups restricted to a single grade of the same sex, it may be said the tests adequately satisfy the criterion of high reliability.

THE PROCEDURE

In any study the methods of analyzing the data are, of course, those which are most likely to yield a definite answer to the basic problem of the investigation. In the present study the basic problem was to determine whether a general ability factor changes as age increases and, if so, in what direction. An answer to this problem could not be obtained unless three subproblems were considered and resolved: (1) a general factor must be identified; (2) some means of measuring the general factor must be determined; (3) measures of the general factor must be compared for different age levels. The procedure of this experiment was concerned with the solution of these three subproblems.

IDENTIFICATION OF A GENERAL FACTOR

It has been stated earlier that the general factor sought in this study was one akin to general power or general ability. It is conceived as the underlying common core of a number of different abilities. It is consequently something which is not measured directly but has to be extracted from the relationships among the different abilities selected for study. One of the well-known methods for determining the extent of relationship among abilities is the computation of coefficients of correlation. This method demonstrates the extent of common variance among variables or tests but it does not go far enough to identify a new variable which may be considered common to the several measures. Factor analysis is an extension of correlation analysis which redescribes the relationships existing among variables (the correlation coefficients) in terms of new hypothetical variables. The new variables or factors represent what is common to a number of the old variables. "A number of the old variables" may mean anything from one (when the factor is called "a specific factor") to all (when the factor is called "a general factor"). In this study, then, the methods of factor analysis would be used to extract a factor representing what was common to all of the different measures—a factor which would then represent the underlying common core of power among the measures.

The general factor was thus a new variable the influence of which was to be studied at different age levels. This plan presupposed that the general factor would be the *same* variable for the different age levels. If five general factors were determined, one for each of the five age levels, any comparisons among them would become comparisons among five somewhat different variables. A more satisfactory procedure is to obtain one general factor for all the age levels and to determine what happens to it as age increases. In this way the analysis deals with the same variable throughout the age range rather than with five different variables which have the same name. The writer therefore decided to use a combined group of all ages as the basic group on which the factor analysis was to be made. The number of cases at each age level was kept the same so that no level was unduly favored by its size.

The decision to use a combined-age group established the framework for the procedure of identifying the general factor. It was now necessary to fill in the details. Included among these details were the problems of determining what measures or variables to analyze, the number of subjects, the question of sex differences, and the kind of factor analysis.

Variables to Be Analyzed

The measures to be analyzed included the eight tests of the Differential Aptitude Tests battery. These had been selected because they were measures of sufficiently different abilities to permit the extraction of a general ability factor. But in dealing with school children, there is always another variable which influences any measures of ability. This variable is the measure of the student's educational maturation—his school experience. One readily obtainable measure of the student's school experience is the grade in which he is registered. Although this variable is highly related to the student's age (the correlation between the two is of the order of .85), it is probably more closely related to measures of ability than is age itself. Since the analysis was to be based on a group including all age levels, the consequent variability in the measure of school maturation (grade) should be sufficient to disclose a considerable relationship between grade and a general ability factor. Indeed, if the measure of school maturation were to fail to show a high relationship with a factor of general ability, then it would be doubtful whether the factor had been properly named. The grade in which the student was registered was therefore included as a ninth variable to aid in the identification of the factor and to contribute another, albeit limited, source of variance.

Size of Sample

The number of cases to be used in a sample usually depends on such practical considerations as the availability of cases and the amount of labor involved in computation, in addition to the primary consideration that the sample be representative of the population. In the present study there was available a very large number of cases from which a sample could be selected. It was therefore decided to use a sample of considerable size to reduce as much as possible errors due to sampling. The group on which the factor analysis was made was therefore set at 1000 cases with 200 cases drawn from each of the five age levels. This group was called the Master Group and was selected from all school systems that had given Form A of the Differential Aptitude Tests to one or more complete grades. One school system, that of Mount Vernon, New York, which had also given Form A, was excluded from the pool out of which the Master Group was drawn.

Combined or Separate Analyses for Boys and Girls

Before the Master Group sample was selected, the question of a separate or combined analysis of boys and girls had to be decided. The manual of the Differential Aptitude Tests presents mean scores of boys and girls on the various tests. An examination of these statistics shows that boys tend to be superior to girls in Mechanical Reasoning and Space Relations, while girls are superior to boys in Spelling, Sentences, and Clerical Speed and Accuracy. Since the two sexes cannot be considered equivalent in ability on the various tests of the battery, it seemed desirable to make the analyses separately for each sex. This has the additional advantage of permitting sex comparisons as well as age comparisons. The Master Group was therefore subdivided into Boys Master Group and Girls Master Group. The number of cases in each of the two Master Groups was retained at 1000 with 200 from each age level.

SELECTION OF CASES

The selection of cases for each of the two Master Groups was made according to the following plan. All students between the ages of 13 and 17 in the twenty-three school systems that had been tested with Form A were distributed according to age and grade. This gave an indication of the percentage of students of each age registered in each of the grades. These data are given in Table II for boys and girls.

TABLE II

GRADE DISTRIBUTION BY SEX AND AGE OF CHILDREN TESTED IN 23 SCHOOL SYSTEMS

| | PERCENTAGE OF BOYS | | | | | | PERCENTAGE OF GIRLS | | | | | |
| Age | Grade | | | | | | Grade | | | | | |
	8	9	10	11	12	N	8	9	10	11	12	N
13	95	5				514	90	10				722
14	39	56	5			1080	33	61	6			1251
15	14	43	40	2		1176	6	38	51	5		1283
16	3	15	41	37	4	1034	1	9	41	43	6	1024
17		4	13	45	37	707		2	9	38	51	730

The 200 cases at each age level of the Master Groups were selected so that they would be representative of the grade distribution for that age. Within each age and grade classification the number of desired cases was worked out according to the percentage distribution shown in Table II. The cases were then selected at random from each age–grade grouping of the combined twenty-three school systems. This procedure was followed for both boys and girls. The two Master Groups, classified according to age and grade, are shown in Table III. The distribution of the Master Groups by school system is given in Table IIIA.

The details of the selection procedure were as follows: For each student in the twenty-three school systems, there was available an

TABLE III

MASTER GROUPS FOR BOYS AND GIRLS CLASSIFIED ACCORDING TO AGE AND GRADE

| Age | NUMBER OF BOYS | | | | | | NUMBER OF GIRLS | | | | | |
| | Grade | | | | | | Grade | | | | | |
	8	9	10	11	12	N	8	9	10	11	12	N
13	190	10				200	180	20				200
14	78	112	10			200	66	122	12			200
15	28	87	80	5		200	12	76	102	10		200
16	6	30	82	74	8	200	2	18	82	86	12	200
17		8	28	90	74	200		4	18	76	102	200

IBM tabulating card which contained the student's test scores, age, grade, sex, school, and a three-digit serial number. The serial numbers started with 001 for each school and corresponded to an alphabetical arrangement of student names within the school. These cards were sorted by age and grade and sex to give the data shown in Table II. By means of the percentages of Table II the 200 cases for each age were apportioned among the various grades (Table III). To select the desired number of cases in any age–grade classification all the cards within that classification were sorted first on a units position of one of the test scores. (The test used was changed from group to group.) This sort disrupted groupings of cards by school system. A second sort was made on the units position of student serial number. Either the odd or the

TABLE IIIA

MASTER GROUPS FOR BOYS AND GIRLS CLASSIFIED ACCORDING TO SCHOOL SYSTEM

City, State	Boys	Girls	City, State	Boys	Girls
Aledo, Ill.	28	21	Jackson, Mich.	10	12
Ann Arbor, Mich.	47	31	Katonah, N. Y.	23	19
Bedford Hills, N. Y.	13	17	Newcastle, Pa.	181	169
Chatham, N. J.	29	32	Pittsburg, Kan.	75	90
Cincinnati, Ohio	31	32	Port Washington, N. Y.	31	20
Columbus, Ohio	42	36	St. Paul, Minn.	126	137
Croton-on-Hudson, N. Y.	33	18	Solvay, N. Y.	62	67
Davenport, Iowa	61	60	Somers, N. Y.	5	9
Dover, N. J.	72	79	Suffern, N. Y.	36	45
Fairmont, Minn.	18	21	Yorktown Heights, N. Y.	10	15
Gering, Nebr.	26	25			
Hamilton, Ohio	41	45	Total	1000	1000

even numbers were then selected until the proper number of cases had been obtained. For some age–grade classifications all student numbers ending with 2, 4, and 6 may have been selected; for others, the selected numbers may have ended with 1, 3, 5, and 7. The final selections thus had no relationship either to school, size of test score, or alphabetical arrangement of cases. Twenty-two of the twenty-three school systems are represented in the final selections for the Master Groups.

The Master Groups were thus made up of subjects from a wide variety of schools and localities and could reasonably be considered typical of children in the age range considered. It might be mentioned at this point that the age–grade classification of students aged 13 appears somewhat restricted. That is to say, one might expect perhaps 15 or 20 per cent of 13-year-olds to be in grades below grade 8. This is doubtless true and would imply that about forty cases at age level 13 should have been in grades below grade 8. However, the effect of forty cases in a group of 1000 is practically negligible, even if it were assumed that they were considerably different from the forty eighth-graders that replaced them. In the comparisons from age to age this kind of restriction becomes more significant and will be considered in greater detail.

Type of Factor Analysis

Having determined the two Master Groups, the problem which remained to complete the identification of the general factor was to decide upon the type of factor analysis to be used. There are several well-known methods of factor-analyzing data. The method of principal components developed by Hotelling was selected because it makes the first factor account for the maximum percentage of the variance. The factor analysis was not stopped after a first factor had been obtained but was continued until a major portion of the variance had been extracted. The factors were then rotated to determine whether greater psychological meaningfulness might be obtained with regard to the first factor. It must be pointed out that the problem of this study is not to get a number of readily identified factors. For this purpose there would be need for several tests of each ability to permit identification. Any rotation of factors based on the variables used here could not conceivably be expected to give more than clues to their identity. However, it might show some changes in the first, or general, factor which would be worthy of investigation. It is this first factor, the common core of all the different abilities being measured, that is the basis of this study.

MEASUREMENT OF THE GENERAL FACTOR

The general factor extracted by the analysis is described in terms of its relationship with each of the nine variables. This relationship is expressed by means of "factor loadings" or estimated coefficients of correlation between the factor and the variables. If different age levels are to be compared on the basis of the general factor, then it is necessary to have some measure of the general factor for each age level. This is the second of the three subproblems, mentioned earlier, which had to be resolved in order to attack the basic problem of the investigation.

It is helpful to note some of the fundamental concepts of factor analysis. A basic assumption is that a score on each of the original variables may be expressed as a linear combination of factor scores after each factor score has been multiplied by the appropriate constant or regression weight. The factors which have been extracted thus represent new variables, on each of which it is theoretically possible to estimate an individual's score. These factor scores, when used with the proper regression coefficients, will predict the scores on the original variables. This is analogous to predicting an individual's score on one test from a knowledge of his scores on a number of other related tests. It follows that, knowing an individual's score on each of the original variables and knowing the relationships between the factors and the variables, it is possible to estimate an individual's score on each factor. Factor scores were thus estimated, and the equations for such computation are given in the next chapter. What is important for the present discussion is that there is a method for computing a "general factor score" for each individual which represents his standing on that variable. Once the factor scores have been obtained, the problem of estimating the general factor has been solved. The general factor scores may then be subjected to various statistical analyses. Mean scores on the general factor may be obtained, as well as correlation coefficients for subgroups between the general factor and the original variables.

It is of course obvious that factor scores may be estimated not only for the general factor but for each of the factors that may be extracted. In this study factor scores were obtained for each of the factors extracted in order to investigate an interesting secondary problem: What are the relationships among factors at different age levels?

The General Factor at Different Age Levels

When a factor has been identified in a factor analysis, it is generally a routine procedure to determine the percentage of variance among the scores which it explains. This percentage may be readily computed and is directly proportional to the sum of the squares of the factor loadings. It may then be said that the factor accounts for a given proportion of the variance, and an estimate of its importance may be made. If several age levels are to be compared with respect to the general factor, a possible approach is to determine the percentage of variance accounted for by the general factor at each age level and base a judgment on these statistics. In some of the studies cited in the preceding chapter, factor analyses were made on each of several age levels, the first factor being extracted and comparisons made among the percentages of variance accounted for by each first factor. This method seems reasonable but has limitations. It has already been noted that separate factor analyses do not yield the same general factors and that comparisons among them are not comparisons which involve the same variables. But aside from this point, a serious limitation of comparing "percentages of variance" is that there is no method for estimating the significance of differences. Unless the differences are very large, so that it is obviously unnecessary to apply tests of significance, it is impossible to determine whether the obtained differences are or are not due to chance.

In the present study, the percentage of variance accounted for by the general factor can be obtained for each age level by the introduction of an intermediate step. To obtain the statistic directly, that is, by the factor loadings, is obviously impossible, since there is only one general factor computed for all the age levels. But after factor scores are computed for each individual it is possible to compute the correlation between each of the original variables and the factor for each age group. These correlation coefficients correspond to the factor loadings and are distinct for each age level. It is then a simple matter to obtain the sum of the squares of these coefficients and compute the percentage of variance accounted for by the general factor at different ages. This gives the percentage of variance for each age level in a satisfactory manner, but there still remains the limitation that the significance of the differences among the percentages cannot be evaluated statistically. However, the intermediate step used in arriving at the percentage of variance results in the computation of correlation coefficients between the original variables and the factor. For every variable there are five correlation coefficients with the factor, corresponding to the five age levels. Comparisons among these five coefficients are possible and may be evaluated statistically. All that is necessary is to change each r to the z-function of Fisher, and the significance of the difference between two coefficients may be computed. If all such comparisons are made within the sets of coefficients between each variable and the general factor, there is a much better basis for estimating the significance of the differences among the percentages of variance accounted for by the general factor at different age levels.

It was therefore decided to make use of two methods in studying the importance of the general factor from age level to age level. The percentages of variance accounted for by the general factor at different age levels would be compared for any general indications of trend; and the examination of percentages would be supplemented by statistical comparisons among the correlation coefficients between the original variables and the general factor.

THE SECONDARY SAMPLE—ALIEN POPULATION

Up to this point, the subjects composing the five age levels between 13 and 17 have not been precisely identified. It would, of course, be possible to obtain factor scores for each member of the Master Group on which the factor analysis was made, arrange the cases by age, and make the comparisons from age to age. By this means the results of the factor analysis would be applied to the cases on which the factor analysis was based. It is a generally recognized principle of good methodology that statistics based on one group be tried out on another group. The second group should be similar in essential characteristics to the first group, but the fact that it is a different group may disclose hidden idiosyncrasies or artifacts of the first set of data. It was therefore decided to construct the regression equations for estimating factor scores on the basis of the analysis of the Master Group and then to obtain factor scores for the individuals of a second group, to be called the "Alien Population." The Alien Population for this study was from the school system of Mount Vernon, New York, which, it was noted earlier, was the one school system excluded from the pool of cases from which the Master Group was selected.

The Differential Aptitude Tests had been given to all children in grades 8 through 12 in the public schools of the city of Mount Vernon. Forms A and B of the battery had been given to alternate halves of the school population for the purpose of comparing the difficulty of the two forms. The Form A data used in this study were thus obtained from a representative sample of the Mount Vernon population in grades 8 through 12.

Mount Vernon is a city of 72,000 people approximately twenty miles from New York City. Some characteristics of Mount Vernon and of the communities included in the Master Group may be obtained from data of the Sixteenth Decennial Census of Population, taken as of April 1, 1940. At that time, the total population of Mount Vernon was approximately 67,000. The median school year completed by the adult population was 9.0. The equivalent statistic computed from data available for seventeen of the twenty-two communities of the Master Group was approximately 9.1. Data with regard to employed workers by major occupation showed that 11 per cent of the Mount Vernon employed people were engaged as professional workers; 14 per cent as proprietors, managers, and officials; 28 per cent as clerical, sales, and kindred workers; and 7 per cent as service workers (not including domestics).[1] The corresponding percentages for urban populations of

[1] All the statistics cited are taken from "Population, Second Series, Characteristics of the Population" for Illinois, Iowa, Kansas, Michigan, Minnesota, Nebraska, New Jersey, New York, Ohio, and Pennsylvania—16th Census of the United States, 1940.

the ten states represented in the Master Group are approximately 8 per cent, 10 per cent, 24 per cent, and 10 per cent. With regard to median school year completed by adults, Mount Vernon's median is almost the same as that of the Master Group; with regard to employed population data, Mount Vernon is somewhat superior to the average of the ten states included in the Master Group. However, the differences are not of such magnitude as to lead to a belief that the *school population* of Mount Vernon is atypical or unlike the school population in the communities of the Master Group. The added fact that in Mount Vernon many of the families of higher income level send their children to private schools (not included in this study) strengthens the belief that its public school sample is not unduly superior to the average public school population.

The most important method for determining whether a group is comparable or similar to another group is consideration of what is known or can be found out about the two groups. From what could be determined about Mount Vernon, it seemed entirely reasonable to accept its school population as being representative of the standardization population of the Differential Aptitude Tests, which, in turn, may be considered representative of children in the section of the country where the tests were given. The entire city of Mount Vernon was sampled to secure the data used in this study, so that there was no loading with very bright or very dull subjects. In all, the Alien Population (Mount Vernon) included essentially the same types of children as the Master Group.

Although statistical tests do not permit one to say that two groups of subjects are similar because the same statistics apply to both, nevertheless serious doubts arise if the same statistics do *not* apply to both. In other words, a statistical test may deny an assumption of similarity even though it cannot positively confirm it. It was decided therefore to apply a statistical test to the Alien Population to see if the assumption of similarity to the Master Group would be denied. This test will be described in detail in Chapter 4. It was found that the results were compatible with the assumption of similarity.

The subjects of the Alien Population were drawn from the two high schools and the four junior high schools of Mount Vernon. Table IV shows the classification of subjects according to age and sex.

TABLE IV

COMPOSITION OF ALIEN POPULATION (MOUNT VERNON, N. Y.) BY AGE AND SEX

Age		Number of Boys	Number of Girls
13		140	120
14		136	151
15		214	201
16		139	181
17		108	133
	Total	737	786

As there were two Master Groups, one for each sex, so there were two corresponding Alien Populations. Comparisons of the importance of the general factor at different age levels were thus based on the cases of two Alien Populations after the "working tools," so to speak, were determined from two Master Groups.

4

THE PRESENTATION OF THE DATA

BEFORE the factor analyses of the Master Groups could be undertaken, it was necessary to compute the intercorrelations among
the eight test variables and grade placement. The Pearson prod-
uct-moment intercorrelations for the Boys and Girls Master Groups
are given in Table V, together with the means and standard deviations of each variable. It will be noted that there is remarkable
similarity between corresponding coefficients for the two sexes.
Of the thirty-six pairs of coefficients only eleven differ by as much
as .05, and of these only two (Grade and Numerical, Grade and
Mechanical) differ by more than .10. The standard deviations of
variables for the two sexes are also very similar but the picture
changes when the mean scores are examined. On Space Relations
and Mechanical Reasoning the boys show a markedly higher mean
score while the girls are superior on Clerical Speed and Accuracy,
Spelling, and Sentences. A hypothesis which suggests itself is that
although the two sexes may differ in level of achievement on some
variables, the relationships which exist among the variables are
substantially the same for both sexes.

Table V contains the basic data for the factor analyses of the
Master Groups. Hotelling's method of principal components [15]
was the statistical procedure used.

The factor analysis of the Boys Master Group was carried
through until 81 per cent of the variance of the scores had been
explained. Four orthogonal factors were extracted, the fourth one
accounting for 7 per cent of the variance. A fifth factor would
have explained less than 7 per cent of the remaining variance—
probably less than 5 per cent. The analysis was therefore stopped
after the loadings for the fourth factor were computed. In the

TABLE V

INTERCORRELATIONS AMONG THE DIFFERENTIAL APTITUDE TESTS AND GRADE PLACEMENT

	Verbal Reasoning	Numerical Ability	Abstract Reasoning	Space Relations	Mechanical Reasoning	Clerical Speed and Accuracy	Spelling	Sentences	Grade Placement
BOYS MASTER GROUP $N = 1000$									
Numerical Ability	.6317								
Abstract Reasoning	.5881	.5655							
Space Relations	.5800	.5412	.5924						
Mechanical Reasoning	.5985	.4735	.5139	.5896					
Clerical Speed and Accuracy	.3033	.3478	.2620	.2883	.2248				
Spelling	.6013	.4422	.3250	.3052	.3204	.2877			
Sentences	.7213	.5570	.4999	.4585	.4737	.3361	.6775		
Grade Placement	.4395	.3301	.2889	.3017	.3518	.4606	.3982	.4656	
Mean	21.88	18.42	26.60	44.38	38.05	49.32	37.98	29.89	9.48
S.D.	9.96	9.00	10.96	25.07	13.02	11.61	26.49	16.63	1.30
Maximum Possible Score	50	40	50	100	68	100	100	95	
GIRLS MASTER GROUP $N = 1000$									
Numerical Ability	.5942								
Abstract Reasoning	.6203	.5396							
Space Relations	.5567	.4685	.5759						
Mechanical Reasoning	.5536	.4296	.5042	.5774					
Clerical Speed and Accuracy	.3526	.2725	.2777	.2655	.1703				
Spelling	.6023	.4045	.3822	.2712	.2537	.3859			
Sentences	.7437	.5405	.5251	.4379	.4345	.3739	.6762		
Grade Placement	.4313	.1208	.2221	.2322	.2218	.4570	.4698	.4868	
Mean	21.43	17.15	24.47	37.29	23.18	56.74	50.75	36.93	9.64
S.D.	9.59	8.09	11.47	21.59	10.94	12.46	26.35	16.69	1.33
Maximum Possible Score	50	40	50	100	68	100	100	95	

case of the Girls Master Group four orthogonal factors again accounted for 81 per cent of the variance, with the fourth one accounting for 7 per cent. This analysis was also stopped after four factors had been extracted. The factor loadings of each factor for the two Master Groups are presented, to three decimal places, in Table VI.

TABLE VI

Unrotated Factor Loadings for the Two Master Groups

Variable	I	II	BOYS III	IV	h^2	I	II	GIRLS III	IV	h^2
Verbal Reasoning	.868	−.069	−.200	.039	.800	.881	−.033	−.133	.107	.806
Numerical Ability	.770	−.137	.016	−.364	.744	.705	−.290	−.296	−.372	.807
Abstract Reasoning	.731	−.358	.136	−.173	.711	.748	−.314	.023	−.121	.673
Space Relations	.732	−.377	.253	.031	.743	.697	−.390	.351	.015	.761
Mechanical Reasoning	.715	−.324	.138	.420	.812	.659	−.419	.281	.303	.781
Clerical Speed and Accuracy	.502	.530	.541	−.295	.913	.523	.481	.404	−.535	.954
Spelling	.679	.332	−.520	−.067	.846	.705	.400	−.381	.072	.807
Sentences	.819	.159	−.331	−.013	.806	.840	.172	−.261	.120	.818
Grade Placement	.600	.519	.218	.422	.855	.545	.615	.284	.325	.861
Percentage of Variance	52	12	10	7		50	15	9	7	

The corresponding factor loadings of the four factors for the two sexes are strikingly similar. This, of course, would have been expected from the great similarity of the tables of intercorrelations for boys and girls. With regard to the first two factors, the greatest differences between loadings for the two sexes are .065 for the first factor (Numerical Ability loadings) and .153 for the second factor (Numerical Ability loadings). The third factor shows a greater difference between Numerical Ability loadings of boys and girls, .306, and somewhat larger differences between the Mechanical Reasoning, Clerical Speed and Accuracy, and Spelling loadings of the two sexes (of the order of .14). The fourth factor loadings show the greatest difference in Clerical Speed and Accuracy, .24. On the whole, the factor loadings for the two sexes and the percentages of variance accounted for by each factor for each sex show remarkable similarity rather than any striking differences.

The first factor is of particular interest in this study. In the case of both boys and girls it is by far the most important factor, accounting for more than half of the total variance. For both sexes, its lowest loading is on Clerical Speed and Accuracy, the only test of the battery given under speed conditions. However, even the loading of the Clerical test exceeds .500. The loadings of the eight Differential Aptitude Tests on the first factor are high for both sexes. Grade Placement, which would be expected to have a relatively high correlation with general ability, has a loading on the first factor of .600 for boys and .545 for girls. In view of the loadings of each of the nine variables, it seems reasonable to consider the first factor a general ability factor.

Inspection of the tests may lead to a more precise name than "general ability factor." Although the test content differs considerably from test to test, the uniformly high loadings of the first factor indicate something common to all of them. The tests are, with the exception of the Clerical test, measures of power rather than speed. Three of the tests, Verbal Reasoning, Abstract Reasoning, and Mechanical Reasoning, call for reasoning in various types of situations. The Numerical Ability test actually calls for reasoning with numerical relationships. The Space Relations test, which requires visualization and mental manipulation of three-dimensional objects after looking at a two-dimensional pattern, also entails reasoning power. The Sentences test calls for recognition of proper and improper grammatical usage in parts of sentences. Although it cannot be maintained that this is reasoning ability in the sense of the other tests, nevertheless some kind of reasoning is involved in going from the meaning of a sentence to a determination of the grammatical accuracy of its parts. The Spelling and Clerical tests are essentially tests of recognition of the correct stimulus with the latter test placing a great premium on speed. These two tests probably reflect rote skills and accuracy of perception more than anything else. But on the whole the first factor may be associated more with power than with speed, and probably with general reasoning ability. Although the speeded Clerical test has the lowest loading on the first factor, it still has a high loading for both sexes. This seems to indicate that speed is to a certain extent associated with the first factor. It is true that power tests keep speed to a minimum but it is doubtful that they eliminate it entirely. In summary, the first factor may be said to represent general reasoning power to a large extent and speed and rote knowledge to a much lesser degree.

It is noteworthy that not only the first factors, but also the factor patterns, are very much alike for the two sexes. An outstanding feature of Table VI is the preponderance of small differences between factor loadings for boys and girls. Although there are sex differences in level of achievement on some tests, the tables of intercorrelations among the tests and the factor patterns for the sexes are very similar.

ROTATION OF FACTORS

The primary purpose of the rotation of each factorial pattern was to obtain a new first factor which was more definitely associated with power and with reasoning ability than the unrotated first factor. To this end the Clerical Speed and Accuracy test loading and the Grade Placement loading were reduced. By reducing the weight of the Clerical test the factor comes closer to being a power measure; by reducing the weight of Grade Placement the factor is less influenced by school experience and school maturation. The rotated first factor is then more of a power measure of reasoning ability or intelligence than the unrotated first factor. The supposition that the general factor is closely allied to reasoning power is supported if the purer measure of reasoning power (the rotated first factor) yields results similar to those for the general factor. In keeping with a rotated first factor that would be essentially reasoning power, the loading of the Spelling Test was also reduced. The rotations were thus made in order to reduce the loadings of Clerical Speed and Accuracy, Grade Placement, and Spelling, while keeping the loadings on the "reasoning" variables at a high level.

The writer experiences a certain amount of trepidation in using the word "reasoning" to describe the general factor. It is not intended to convey the thought that either the unrotated or rotated first factor is a psychological entity for which the term "reasoning" is an apt description. "Reasoning" is here used in a general sense to identify a factor extracted from tests in which some form of reasoning ability is required. It is hoped that the label will serve to distinguish this kind of general factor from one derived from tests which emphasize speed or memory or recognition of stimuli rather than some form of reasoning.

Another consideration which conditioned the rotations was that the rotated structure should remain orthogonal and the loadings positive, in so far as possible. In dealing with orthogonal structures there is the distinct advantage of knowing that all factors bear the same relationship to each other—in effect, zero relationship. When the results of the analysis are applied to different groups, the interrelationships among factors may change. But it should be easier to identify and possibly to explain such changes if the reference frame is orthogonal. The condition that the loadings remain positive, in so far as this is possible while satisfying the condition of orthogonality of factors, is consistent with a concept of positive relationship among mental abilities. It seems to the writer that negative correlations, as expressed by negative loadings, between mental tests and their basic factors are psychologically inexplainable.

The conditions placed upon the first factor, and the maintenance of orthogonality and positive loadings, resulted in the rotated patterns presented in Table VII. The original factors, as axes, were rotated graphically, two at a time. For the boys, factors I and II were rotated through 40° to obtain new axes I' and II'. The second rotation was 37° for axes II' and III and the final rotation was 50° for axes III' and IV. The final axes or rotated factors have the loadings given in Table VII. For the girls, it was found necessary to do five rotations to bring the final structure into line with the conditions that had been set up. The original factors I and II were rotated through 48° to the new axes I' and II'. The axes II' and III were rotated through 63° to get II" and III'. A rotation of 43° for axes III' and IV resulted in III" and IV'. The axes

II″ and III″ were rotated through 62° to get II‴ and III‴ and II‴ and IV′ through 57° to get II″″ and IV″. The final orthogonal axes, the rotated factors, are given in Table VII.

TABLE VII

ROTATED FACTOR LOADINGS FOR THE TWO MASTER GROUPS

Variable	I	II	BOYS III	IV	h^2	I	II	GIRLS III	IV	h^2
Verbal Reasoning	.611	.534	.272	.263	.802	.677	.485	.302	.150	.807
Numerical Ability	.600	.289	−.015	.549	.745	.718	.251	−.150	.454	.807
Abstract Resaoning	.744	.090	.090	.376	.711	.766	.113	.154	.223	.673
Space Relations	.759	−.011	.285	.291	.742	.779	−.132	.367	.053	.762
Mechanical Reasoning	.708	.094	.549	.001	.812	.770	−.020	.368	−.226	.780
Clerical Speed and Accuracy	−.083	.004	.356	.883	.913	.067	−.011	.591	.776	.956
Spelling	.182	.857	.124	.252	.846	.256	.777	.249	.275	.807
Sentences	.405	.704	.237	.303	.808	.509	.658	.297	.194	.818
Grade Placement	−.012	.303	.815	.315	.855	−.007	.421	.826	.052	.862
Percentage of Variance	28	20	15	18		34	17	18	12	

It must be emphasized that these are the rotations of the writer, who set up definite conditions for rotating the factors. He used his own judgment for determining which of several rotations would be acceptable. Another investigator might have set different conditions or possibly obtained somewhat different results even with the same conditions. The essential points for this study are that the rotated structures present a first factor which may be used as a check on the general unrotated first factor, and that the relationships among rotated factors as well as among unrotated factors may be investigated for different age groups.

Examination of Table VII shows considerable similarity between the rotated factors of boys and girls. The first factor, for both sexes, seems to be a measure of general reasoning power. No attempt will be made to name the remaining factors. Such attempts might yield reasonable names, but it is restated here that this problem is not properly set up for identification of factors and attempts at naming are merely rough speculations. It will be noted, however, that the factors for the two sexes show considerable correspondence with regard to the variables exhibiting the highest loadings. The percentage of variance accounted for by each rotated factor is recorded in Table VII. These percentages are noted principally for checking purposes. Since they are completely dependent upon the manner of rotation, they no longer have the same meaning as the percentages for the unrotated factors (Table VI).

Tables VI and VII, the unrotated and rotated factor loadings, constitute the basic factor analysis data of the Master Groups. For both sexes, the unrotated first factor may be considered a general factor closely allied with reasoning ability and the rotated first factor may be considered a purer power measure of general reasoning. Both the rotated and the unrotated structures for boys and girls are orthogonal and account for a major portion, 81 per cent, of the variance of the scores.

ESTIMATION OF FACTOR SCORES

The next step in the analysis was to determine factor scores for each individual in the Alien Population and to compare various statistics at the different age levels. Factor scores were therefore estimated for the unrotated first factor (the general factor) and for the rotated first factor (reasoning power). However, a secondary problem with interesting implications was to determine what happens to the relationships among factors when each age level is considered separately. The four unrotated and the four rotated factors based on the Master Groups are orthogonal to each other. Since the Master Groups include all five age levels, it is entirely possible that the orthogonality will not be maintained when the same factors are studied for a single age level. That is to say, orthogonal factors derived from a widespread age sample may become related when applied to a homogeneous age sample. There may also be different relationships at different ages. To investigate this problem it was decided to estimate factor scores for all of the obtained factors, rotated and unrotated, and to obtain the intercorrelations among factors at the various age levels.

The groups for which the age-to-age comparisons were made were the Alien Populations, children in the school system of Mount Vernon, New York. The regression equations for estimating the factor scores were based on the Master Groups and applied to the Alien Populations. The problem of determining factor scores from an analysis of the Hotelling type is relatively simple. Roughly, it is the sum of the products of factor loadings and test scores [15]. The actual equation for a given factor score is

$$\text{Factor Score} = \Sigma \, a_{pj} \, x_{ji}$$

where a_{pj} is the unrotated Hotelling loading on factor p divided by the standard deviation of the Master Group for variable j, and x_{ji} is the score of individual i on variable j (j covers the nine original variables). The unrotated factor loadings of Table VI were accordingly made into the a_{pj} values of the equation. These values, for each of the unrotated factors, are given in Table VIII.

TABLE VIII

VALUES OF REGRESSION COEFFICIENTS (a_{pj}) FOR UNROTATED FACTORS

Variable	BOYS				GIRLS			
	I	II	III	IV	I	II	III	IV
Verbal Reasoning	.0871	−.0069	−.0201	.0039	.0919	−.0034	−.0139	.0112
Numerical Ability	.0855	−.0152	.0018	−.0404	.0872	−0359	−.0366	−.0460
Abstract Reasoning	.0667	−.0326	.0124	−.0158	.0652	−.0274	.0020	−.0106
Space Relations	.0292	−.0150	.0101	.0012	.0323	−.0181	.0163	.0007
Mechanical Reasoning	.0549	−.0249	.0106	.0323	.0602	−.0383	.0257	.0277
Clerical Speed and Accuracy	.0432	.0456	.0466	−.0254	.0420	.0386	.0324	−.0430
Spelling	.0256	.0125	−.0196	−.0025	.0268	.0152	−.0145	.0027
Sentences	.0492	.0096	−.0199	−.0008	.0503	.0103	−.0156	.0072
Grade Placement	.4624	.4000	.1680	.3252	.4087	.4612	.2130	.2430

The multiplications and additions of the formula were then carried out for every individual in the Alien Population to yield factor scores on each of the four unrotated factors.

To estimate factor scores for the rotated factors, it is necessary to introduce the inverse of the original correlation matrix into the regression equations. The general formula may be written as

$$\text{Rotated Factor Score}_p = \Sigma \, w_{pj} \, x_{ji}$$

The values, w_{pj}, are the results of post-multiplying the row vectors of rotated factor loadings by the inverse of the original correlation matrix and dividing the elements of the resulting row vectors by the test standard deviations of the Master Group.[1] The computation of the inverse matrix for each Master Group was accomplished by the method described by Tucker [27] in *Psychometrika*. The inverse matrices for the Boys and Girls Master Groups are given in Table IX. The values, w_{pj}, are presented for each rotated factor in Table X. In the equation for rotated factor scores the values of x_{ji} are, as before, the scores of the individuals of the Alien Populations on each of the nine original variables. In this way, factor scores on each of the four rotated factors were estimated for every subject in the Alien Populations. After the factor scores had been estimated, correlations among factors and between factors and original tests could be computed for age levels.

ORTHOGONALITY OF FACTORS IN ALIEN POPULATIONS

It has been noted earlier that there was reason to believe the Alien Populations (the boys and girls of the Mount Vernon school system) constituted the same types of populations as the Master Groups. As a further check on this belief the following question was posed: Do the rotated and unrotated factors, which are independent for the Master Groups, remain independent factors for the Alien Populations? A positive answer to the question does not, in and of itself, establish the similarity of the two population samples. It simply does not *deny* the supposition of similarity and in that way is compatible with such a supposition. A negative answer to the question, however, would raise doubts as to the applicability of the statistics of one group to the other group.

[1] A derivation of the formula is given in the Appendix.

TABLE IX

INVERSE OF CORRELATION MATRIX FOR EACH MASTER GROUP

	Verbal Reasoning	Numerical Ability	Abstract Reasoning	Space Relations	Mechanical Reasoning	Clerical Speed and Accuracy	Spelling	Sentences	Grade Placement
BOYS									
Verbal Reasoning	3.1864								
Numerical Ability	-.5258	2.0057							
Abstract Reasoning	-.3851	-.4124	1.9390						
Space Relations	-.3705	-.3062	-.5214	2.0270					
Mechanical Reasoning	-.5757	-.0651	-.2075	-.5736	1.8743				
Clerical Speed and Accuracy	.1226	-.2485	-.0350	-.1457	.0801	1.3636			
Spelling	-.5985	-.1280	.1712	.1328	.1401	-.0711	2.0249		
Sentences	-.9163	-.2246	-.2479	-.0110	-.0989	-.0760	-.9894	2.7896	
Grade Placement	-.1927	.0732	.0380	.0241	-.1986	-.5101	-.1465	-.2831	1.5370
GIRLS									
Verbal Reasoning	3.3206								
Numerical Ability	-.4985	1.8826							
Abstract Reasoning	-.5139	-.3201	1.9990						
Space Relations	-.3594	-.1946	-.5044	1.9157					
Mechanical Reasoning	-.4995	-.1192	-.2189	-.5822	1.7657				
Clerical Speed and Accuracy	.0309	-.1912	-.0930	-.1407	.1194	1.3916			
Spelling	-.5256	-.1234	-.0330	.1979	.2053	-.1950	2.0995		
Sentences	-1.0586	-.4205	-.1845	-.0051	-.1074	-.0034	-.9012	2.9948	
Grade Placement	-.3155	.4805	.1298	-.0514	-.0767	-.5061	-.3011	-.4597	1.6748

TABLE X

VALUES OF REGRESSION COEFFICIENTS (w_{pj}) FOR ROTATED FACTORS

Variable	BOYS				GIRLS			
	I	II	III	IV	I	II	III	IV
Verbal Reasoning	.0169	.0250	.0013	−.0085	.0170	.0258	−.0005	−.0095
Numerical Ability	.0224	.0013	−.0479	.0469	.0327	.0067	−.0580	.0601
Abstract Reasoning	.0319	−.0165	−.0188	.0181	.0247	−.0108	−.0066	.0119
Space Relations	.0146	−.0119	.0040	.0015	.0145	−.0181	.0118	−.0037
Mechanical Reasoning	.0252	−.0132	.0424	−.0320	.0293	−.0183	.0271	−.0441
Clerical Speed and Accuracy	−.0263	−.0227	.0068	.0726	−.0128	−.0328	.0298	.0692
Spelling	−.0053	.0251	−.0060	−.0009	−.0034	.0226	−.0040	.0022
Sentences	.0001	.0267	−.0027	−.0013	.0030	.0264	−.0026	−.0036
Grade Placement	−.2196	.0324	.6428	−.0601	−.1687	.1237	.5084	−.1972

Since the factor scores were now available, it was possible to compute the intercorrelations among the factors. If these coefficients are reasonably close to zero, then the factors may be considered essentially independent for both the Master Groups and the Alien Populations. The Master Groups had included equal numbers of cases at each of the five age levels. Samples of the Alien Populations were therefore selected to include the same proportion of cases at each age level. The age and grade distributions of the Alien Populations are given in Table XI.

TABLE XI

THE ALIEN POPULATIONS BY AGE AND GRADE

Age	NUMBER OF BOYS						NUMBER OF GIRLS					
	Grade					*N*	Grade					*N*
	8	9	10	11	12		8	9	10	11	12	
13	108	31	1			140	88	32				120
14	43	74	19			136	31	94	26			151
15	29	66	98	20	1	214	15	38	106	40	2	201
16	1	15	46	57	20	139	3	10	33	101	34	181
17		5	15	30	58	108		1	13	30	89	133

For both boys and girls, 100 cases were selected from each age level to correspond to the grade distribution for that age. The method of selecting cases was the same as that used to select the Master Groups. Thus, two samples, each of which included 500 cases, were drawn from the Alien Populations.

The coefficients of correlation among the unrotated and rotated factors are presented for each sample in Table XII. Inspection of the table reveals that the coefficients are low. In a sample

TABLE XII

INTERCORRELATIONS AMONG FACTORS IN SAMPLES OF ALIEN POPULATIONS

| | UNROTATED FACTORS | | | | | ROTATED FACTORS | | | |
	I	II	III	IV		I	II	III	IV
				Boys Sample (N = 500)					
II	.036				II	.135			
III	−.110	.114			III	−.043	−.109		
IV	−.149	−.152	.035		IV	−.076	.116	−.030	
				Girls Sample (N = 500)					
II	.041				II	.115			
III	−.089	.034			III	.200	.044		
IV	−.182	.022	−.044		IV	−.018	.005	.118	

of 500 cases a coefficient would not be considered significantly different from zero at the 1 per cent level unless it exceeded .115. Of the twelve coefficients presented for boys only four exceed this value; for girls, only three of the twelve coefficients exceed .115. The highest coefficient in the table is .200, between rotated factors I and III for girls. This indicates only 4 per cent of common variance between the two factors. In light of the very low correlation coefficients among the factors it may reasonably be said that the orthogonal structure of the Master Groups was essentially maintained in the Alien Populations. The results of this test are compatible with the basic supposition that the Master Groups and Alien Population are similar and that the statistics of the former groups may reasonably be applied to the latter. Subsequent analyses were made on the total Alien Population.

COMPARISON OF PERCENTAGES OF VARIANCE

The first investigation of the general factor was the comparison of the percentages of variance accounted for by the first factor at different age levels. As has been noted earlier, the percentage of variance may be computed from the correlation coefficients between the original variables and the first factor, squaring and adding these coefficients and dividing by 9. The correlation coefficients between the factor and original variables are estimates of the loadings of the variables on the factor; the 9 represents the sum of the variances of the nine variables.

Table XIII shows the correlation coefficients between the original variables and the general factor together with the percentage of variance accounted for by the general factor at each age level of the two Alien Populations. Inspection of the "Percentage of Variance" entries of Table XIII discloses three things worthy of note. The percentages of variance explained by the general factor at the various age levels are remarkably similar for the two sexes; the percentage for age 13 is considerably lower than that of any other age; the percentages for ages 14 through 17 remain very similar and do not show any tendency to decrease or to increase.

The "behavior" of age level 13, for both sexes, seems strange and merits further investigation. A clue to a reasonable explanation is furnished by the correlation between Grade Placement and the general factor at age 13. For both boys and girls this coefficient is very much lower than the corresponding coefficients at other age levels. This seems to indicate restriction in the grade range of 13-year-olds, a fact which would account for lower correlations. Since the subjects of this study were children tested in grades 8 through 12, it is entirely possible that a sizable proportion of 13-year-olds were not included because they were in grades below 8. To estimate the percentage of excluded 13-year-olds, the writer obtained from the Mount Vernon school system tables of enrollment by age and grade of the entire system for 1946 and 1947. These tables showed that approximately 25 per cent of 13-year-old children were below the eighth grade. The percentage of 14-year-old children not included in testing grades 8 through 12 was about 6 per cent; for 15-, 16-, and 17-year-olds the percent-

TABLE XIII

CORRELATIONS BETWEEN ORIGINAL VARIABLES AND GENERAL FACTOR AND
PERCENTAGE OF VARIANCE EXPLAINED BY GENERAL FACTOR FOR
ALIEN POPULATIONS AT EACH AGE LEVEL

| Variable | BOYS | | | | | GIRLS | | | | |
| | r with Age | | | | | r with Age | | | | |
	13	14	15	16	17	13	14	15	16	17
Verbal Reasoning	.858	.898	.883	.928	.919	.856	.889	.882	.904	.892
Numerical Ability	.802	.846	.822	.804	.884	.735	.818	.860	.841	.834
Abstract Reasoning	.770	.809	.827	.807	.820	.740	.850	.849	.799	.824
Space Relations	.733	.723	.653	.720	.669	.581	.696	.713	.688	.729
Mechanical Reasoning	.648	.698	.695	.715	.634	.570	.673	.733	.704	.702
Clerical Speed and Accuracy	.135	.474	.525	.560	.395	.413	.534	.635	.482	.498
Spelling	.743	.769	.693	.778	.774	.606	.759	.723	.682	.714
Sentences	.860	.877	.874	.875	.814	.777	.870	.887	.865	.879
Grade Placement	.443	.690	.727	.682	.644	.309	.706	.697	.609	.631
Percentage of Variance	49	58	57	59	55	41	58	61	55	57

age was 1 per cent or less. It thus appears that a sizable group of presumably less able children was not included among the 13-year-old children of this study. This would have the effect of lowering the correlation coefficients for 13-year-olds since the group is more restricted with regard to ability. The percentage of variance accounted for by the first factor, a function of the correlation coefficients between the original variables and the factor, would consequently be lower than it should be. It is therefore necessary to consider the percentage of variance for age level 13 as an underestimate. Had a larger proportion of the less able 13-year-old children been included in the study, it is likely that the percentage of variance accounted for by the general factor at age 13 would be more in line with the percentages obtained for the other age levels.

The safest conclusion with regard to the percentages of variance accounted for by the general factor at various age levels seems to be that there is no substantial change with increase in age. If there is any tendency indicated at all, it appears to be toward an increase with age. Some of the brighter 17-year-olds were not in secondary schools at the time of testing. To that extent there is restriction in the range of ability of the 17-year-old groups, and the correlations may possibly have been underestimated. However, the coefficients for the 17-year-old groups show no tendency to be lower than those of younger groups, and the most reasonable general conclusion would seem to be that there is no tendency for the percentages of variance accounted for by the general factor to change markedly in the age range considered. Once again, the data for the two sexes are very similar.

COMPARISONS OF CORRELATION COEFFICIENTS

Since there is no available formula for the standard error of a percentage of variance, there can be no statistical test of the significance of a difference between two percentages of variance. An investigator is forced to use subjective judgment to determine whether or not one percentage of variance is reliably different from another percentage. In the data discussed in the foregoing section, percentage differences seemed quite small to the writer and he assumed that the differences were not significant. Confirmation of such judgment by objective means is highly desirable. An approach to the problem of confirmation becomes apparent after consideration of the manner in which the percentages of variance were computed. It will be recalled that the correlation coefficients between the original variables and the general factor served as the basic data for obtaining the percentages of variance. For each variable, the correlation coefficients with the general factor are available for the five age levels, and comparisons among them may be made. These comparisons are simply the comparisons of two independent correlation coefficients, and the method developed by Fisher [9] is applicable. Each coefficient may be transformed to z, the standard error of z can readily be determined, and the ratio of the difference between z's to the standard error of the difference may be computed and interpreted. By the intercomparisons of correlation coefficients, each variable which entered into the percentage of variance may be investigated. These comparisons aid in determining the influence of the general factor at different age levels. The same type of investigation may be undertaken with the rotated first factor, reasoning power. Comparisons may then be made of changes with age in the relationships between the general factor and the original variables and between the reasoning power factor and the original variables.

Tables XIV (for boys) and XV (for girls) present the z-function equivalents of the correlation coefficients between original variables and the general and reasoning power factors, along with critical ratios of the differences between coefficients for different age levels.

If the ratio of the difference between z's to the standard error of the difference is equal to 2.58, then the difference between the compared correlation coefficients is significant at the 1 per cent level of confidence. That is, the chances are only one in one hundred that the correlation coefficients were computed on samples of equally correlated populations. Throughout this study, a difference significant at the 1 per cent level has been considered indicative of a real difference. Thus, in Tables XIV and XV a ratio which equals or exceeds 2.58 is taken to indicate a real difference, while a ratio lower than 2.58 is attributed to chance. With this criterion in mind, it will be noted that of the ninety differences between corresponding correlation coefficients with the general factor for different age levels, only seven are significant for the boys and nine for the girls. Each of these significant differences is between a 13-year-old group and an older group, with the correlation coefficient higher for the older group. It was pointed out earlier that there is probably restriction in the 13-year-old group since a sizable proportion of the children in grades below the eighth were not included. This may account for the lower correlation coefficients at age 13 and the consequent significant differences when comparisons are made with older groups. But temporarily disregarding comparisons with age 13, it is apparent that there is no significant change between each variable and the general factor as age increases. If there is any indication of trend at all it seems to be toward a slight increase in relationship with increasing age.

The correlation coefficients between the rotated factor, reasoning power, and the original variables also appear in Tables XIV and XV along with the significance of differences in relationships among the various age levels. The picture presented by the differences in correlations with reasoning power is essentially no different from that presented by the differences in coefficients with the general factor. For boys, four of the ninety differences in cor-

TABLE XIV

COMPARISONS AMONG CORRELATIONS BETWEEN ORIGINAL VARIABLES AND GENERAL AND REASONING POWER FACTORS

BOYS ALIEN POPULATION

Variable	Age	N	GENERAL FACTOR						REASONING POWER FACTOR					
			r_{iG}	z_{iG}	Ratio of Difference to Standard Error*				r_{iR}	z_{iR}	Ratio of Difference to Standard Error*			
					13	14	15	16			13	14	15	16
Verbal Reasoning	13	140	.858	1.2857					.637	.7531				
	14	136	.898	1.4618	1.44				.734	.9373	1.51			
	15	214	.883	1.3892	.94	−.65			.624	.7315	−.20	−1.85		
	16	139	.928	1.6438	2.96	1.49	2.31		.724	.9160	1.35	−.17	1.68	
	17	108	.919	1.5826	2.28	.92	1.63	−.47	.692	.8518	.76	−.65	1.01	−.49
Numerical Ability	13	140	.802	1.1042					.639	.7565				
	14	136	.846	1.2419	1.13				.673	.8162	.49			
	15	214	.822	1.1630	.53	−.71			.534	.5957	−1.46	−1.99		
	16	139	.804	1.1098	.05	−1.08	−.48		.593	.6823	−.61	−1.10	.79	
	17	108	.884	1.3938	2.23	1.16	1.94	2.18	.612	.7121	−.34	−.79	.98	.23
Abstract Reasoning	13	140	.770	1.0203					.793	1.0795				
	14	136	.809	1.1241	.85				.770	1.0203	−.49			
	15	214	.827	1.1786	1.44	.49			.761	.9986	−.74	−.20		
	16	139	.807	1.1184	.81	−.05	−.55		.758	.9915	−.73	−.24	−.06	
	17	108	.820	1.1568	1.05	.25	−.18	.30	.782	1.0505	−.22	.23	.44	.45
Space Relations	13	140	.733	.9352					.768	1.0154				
	14	136	.723	.9139	−.17				.804	1.1098	.77			
	15	214	.653	.7805	−1.41	−1.20			.820	1.1568	1.29	.42		
	16	139	.720	.9076	−.23	−.05	1.16		.753	.9798	−.29	−1.07	−1.61	
	17	108	.669	.8089	−.97	−.80	.24	−.76	.798	1.0931	.60	−.13	−.54	.87

Test	Age	N	r	M	vs 13	vs 14	vs 15	vs 16	r	M	vs 13	vs 14	vs 15	vs 16
Mechanical Reasoning	13	140	.648	.7718					.796	1.0876				
	14	136	.698	.8634	.75				.789	1.0688	-.15			
	15	214	.695	.8576	.78	-.05			.804	1.1098	.20	.37		
	16	139	.715	.8975	1.04	.28	.36		.823	1.1661	.65	.80	.51	
	17	108	.634	.7481	-.18	-.88	-.92	-1.15	.813	1.1358	.37	.51	.22	-.23
Clerical Speed and Accuracy	13	140	.135	.1358					-.373	-.3919				
	14	136	.474	.5152	3.11				.021	.0210	-3.38			
	15	214	.525	.5832	4.07	.61			-.015	-.0150	-3.43	-.32		
	16	139	.560	.6328	4.11	.96	.45		.045	.0450	-3.61	.20	.55	
	17	108	.395	.4177	2.17	-.74	-1.39	-1.65	-.092	-.0923	-2.30	.86	.65	1.06
Spelling	13	140	.743	.9571					.389	.4106				
	14	136	.769	1.0179	.50				.382	.4024	-.07			
	15	214	.693	.8537	-.94	-1.48			.214	.2174	-1.76	-1.67		
	16	139	.778	1.0403	.69	.18	1.70		.323	.3350	-.62	-.55	1.07	
	17	108	.774	1.0302	.56	.09	1.48	-.08	.349	.3643	-.36	-.29	1.23	.23
Sentences	13	140	.860	1.2933					.587	.6731				
	14	136	.877	1.3626	.57				.591	.6792	.05			
	15	214	.874	1.3498	.51	-.12			.476	.5178	-1.41	-1.45		
	16	139	.875	1.3540	.50	-.07	.04		.532	.5929	-.66	-.71	.68	
	17	108	.814	1.1388	-1.19	-1.71	-1.77	-1.66	.471	.5114	-1.24	-1.28	-.05	-.68
Grade Placement	13	140	.443	.4760					.076	.0761				
	14	136	.690	.8480	3.05				.381	.4012	2.66			
	15	214	.727	.9223	4.06	.67			.284	.2920	1.96	-.98		
	16	139	.682	.8328	2.95	-.12	-.81		.202	.2048	1.06	-1.61	-.79	
	17	108	.644	.7650	2.22	-.63	-1.32	-.52	.194	.1965	.93	-1.56	-.80	-.06

* Positive ratio indicates higher correlation coefficient for older group; negative ratio, higher coefficient for younger group.

TABLE XV

COMPARISONS AMONG CORRELATIONS BETWEEN ORIGINAL VARIABLES AND GENERAL AND REASONING POWER FACTORS

GIRLS ALIEN POPULATION

Variable	Age	N	GENERAL FACTOR							REASONING POWER FACTOR					
			r_{iG}	z_{iG}	Ratio of Difference to Standard Error*				r_{iR}	z_{iR}	Ratio of Difference to Standard Error*			
					13	14	15	16			13	14	15	16
Verbal Reasoning	13	120	.856	1.2782					.709	.8852				
	14	151	.889	1.4171	1.12				.777	1.0378	1.23			
	15	201	.882	1.3847	.91	−.30			.775	1.0327	1.26	−.05		
	16	181	.904	1.4937	1.81	.69	1.06		.798	1.0931	1.75	.50	.59	
	17	133	.892	1.4316	1.21	.12	.42	−.54	.765	1.0082	.97	−.25	−.22	−.74
Numerical Ability	13	120	.735	.9395					.641	.7599				
	14	151	.818	1.1507	1.70				.766	1.0106	2.02			
	15	201	.860	1.2933	3.02	1.31			.814	1.1388	3.24	1.18		
	16	181	.841	1.2246	2.40	.67	−.67		.808	1.1212	3.04	1.00	−.17	
	17	133	.834	1.2011	2.06	.42	−.82	−.20	.812	1.1329	2.94	1.02	−.05	.10
Abstract Reasoning	13	120	.740	.9505					.761	.9986				
	14	151	.850	1.2562	2.47				.850	1.2562	2.08			
	15	201	.849	1.2526	2.58	−.03			.832	1.1946	1.68	−.57		
	16	181	.799	1.0958	1.22	−1.45	−1.52		.822	1.1630	1.38	−.84	−.31	
	17	133	.824	1.1691	1.72	−.73	−.74	.64	.813	1.1358	1.08	1.00	−.52	−.24
Space Relations	13	120	.581	.6640					.764	1.0058				
	14	151	.696	.8595	1.58				.794	1.0822	.62			
	15	201	.713	.8933	1.96	.31			.851	1.2598	2.17	1.63		
	16	181	.688	.8441	1.51	−.14	−.48		.807	1.1184	.95	.33	−1.37	
	17	133	.729	.9266	2.07	.56	.29	.72	.834	1.2011	1.54	.99	−.52	.72

Test	Age	N	r (I)	z (I)	vs13	vs14	vs15	vs16	r (II)	z (II)	vs13	vs14	vs15	vs16
Mechanical Reasoning	13	120	.570	.6475					.719	.9056				
	14	151	.673	.8162	1.36				.811	1.1299	1.81			
	15	201	.733	.9352	2.46	1.09			.797	1.0903	1.58	−.36		
	16	181	.704	.8752	1.91	.53	−.58		.749	.9707	.55	−1.43	−1.16	
	17	133	.702	.8712	1.76	.46	−.57	−.03	.809	1.1241	1.72	−.05	.30	1.33
Clerical Speed and Accuracy	13	120	.413	.4392					−.003	−.0030				
	14	151	.534	.5957	1.26				.263	.2693	2.20			
	15	201	.635	.7498	2.65	1.41			.315	.3261	2.81	.52		
	16	181	.482	.5256	.73	−.63	−2.18		.207	.2100	1.79	−.53	−1.13	
	17	133	.498	.5467	.85	−.41	−1.80	.18	.191	.1934	1.55	−.63	−1.17	−.14
Spelling	13	120	.606	.7026					.201	.2038				
	14	151	.759	.9939	2.35				.489	.5347	2.67			
	15	201	.723	.9139	1.81	−.73			.418	.4453	2.06	−.82		
	16	181	.682	.8328	1.09	−1.45	−.79		.393	.4153	1.78	−1.08	−.29	
	17	133	.714	.8953	1.52	−.82	−.16	.54	.382	.4024	1.56	−1.10	−.38	−.11
Sentences	13	120	.777	1.0378					.559	.6314				
	14	151	.870	1.3331	2.38				.685	.8385	1.67			
	15	201	.887	1.4077	3.16	.68			.712	.8912	2.22	.48		
	16	181	.865	1.3129	2.31	−.18	−.92		.700	.8673	1.98	.26	−.23	
	17	133	.879	1.3714	2.63	.32	−.32	.51	.710	.8872	2.01	.41	−.04	.17
Grade Placement	13	120	.309	.3194					.032	.0320				
	14	151	.706	.8792	4.51				.500	.5493	4.17			
	15	201	.697	.8614	4.63	−.16			.425	.4538	3.61	−.88		
	16	181	.609	.7073	3.26	−1.55	−1.50		.309	.3194	2.42	−2.07	−1.30	
	17	133	.631	.7431	3.34	−1.13	−1.05	.31	.317	.3283	2.33	−1.84	−1.11	.08

* Positive ratio indicates higher correlation coefficient for older group; negative ratio, higher coefficient for younger group.

relation coefficients between original variables and the reasoning factor are significant, as compared with seven when the correlation is with the general factor. For girls, seven differences between co-efficients with reasoning power are significant, as compared with nine when the correlation is with the general factor. With the reasoning power factor, as with the general factor, all significant differences are between age level 13 and higher levels. Inspection of the correlation coefficients with the reasoning power factor points out a peculiar entry in Table XIV. The coefficient be-tween Clerical Speed and Accuracy and the reasoning power factor is —.373 for age level 13 and considerably lower for the higher age levels. This seems to be a reversal of the usual trend. Considera-tion of the coefficient between Clerical Speed and Accuracy and the general factor shows it to be surprisingly different from the coefficients for the older levels: it is very much lower. It might be reasonable to call these two divergent coefficients "idiosyncrasies of the data." This may even be the best explanation. However, a possible explanation seems to lie in the relationships among the factors at the different age levels. This will be explored in greater detail in the section which deals with the relationships among factors at different age levels.

Aside from the one strange coefficient between Clerical Speed and Accuracy and the reasoning power factor at age 13, all sig-nificant differences show a higher coefficient for the higher age levels. If allowance is again made for the underestimation of the correlation coefficients of the 13-year-old group, then the relation-ships with reasoning power show no significant changes as age in-creases. The status of the reasoning power factor is essentially the same as that of the general factor. This seems to lend support to the idea that the general factor of this study is strongly related to reasoning power in so far as changes in relationships are con-cerned.

A conservative generalization may be made from an over-all view of Tables XIV and XV that there is no indication of change in relationship between the general factor and the original varia-bles over the age range 13–17. The data in these tables support the conclusion which was drawn from the comparison of percentages of variance.

SUMMARY OF FINDINGS CONCERNING THE GENERAL FACTOR

The salient features of the statistical analyses of the general factor may be briefly indicated: (1) The comparisons of the percentages of variance accounted for by the general factor at different age levels show very little change in percentage as age increases. (2) Comparisons among the correlation coefficients between each of the original variables and the general factor give no indication of change in these coefficients as age increases. The relatively few marked changes showed higher coefficients for the older age groups. A parallel comparison of correlation coefficients with the reasoning power factor (rotated factor) reveals the same situation: there were very few significant changes in correlation coefficients as age increased, and these few tended to show higher coefficients for the older groups. With regard to change in relationship with original variables at different age levels, the general factor and the reasoning power factor are very similar. This similarity supports the interpretation of the general factor of this study as one closely allied to reasoning power. (3) None of the analyses disclose any marked differences in results for the two sexes. The similarity of results for boys and girls may be noted in all analyses.

RELATIONSHIPS AMONG FACTORS

A feature of this study has been the investigation of the same general factor at all five age levels. The original factor analysis was made on a Master Group which was heterogeneous as to age. The resulting general factor was then studied at each age level of a second population. This was done separately for each sex. It will be recalled that the factor analysis of each Master Group was continued until four factors had been extracted. These factors were independent, or orthogonal to each other. When the factors were rotated the orthogonality was maintained. The independence of the rotated and unrotated factors was then tested on samples of the Alien Populations. For these samples, which were made up of equal proportions of each of the five age levels to parallel the Master Groups, factor scores were estimated and the intercorrelations among factors were computed. It was found that the Master Group factors remained substantially independent for the Alien Population: the highest correlation between factors, for either sex, was .20. The questions which now arise are: Do these factors which are independent for a widespread age group remain independent at each age level? If not, are there differences between age levels? The answers to these questions were sought for each sex separately.

In order to investigate the relationships among factors at different ages, the intercorrelations among unrotated factor scores and the correlations among rotated factor scores were computed for each age level. These are given in Table XVI. The coefficients marked with an asterisk are significantly different from zero at the 1 per cent level of confidence. For boys, thirteen of the thirty coefficients among unrotated factors are significantly different from zero. Four of these are quite low, below .300, but the other nine represent 10 per cent or more of common variance between factors. For each age level, factors II and IV show a substantial negative correlation. There appear to be differences in factorial relationships not only between each age level and the combined group of age levels but also, to a smaller extent, from age level to age level. Inspection of the coefficients among the rotated factors for boys reveals 11 coefficients significantly different from zero, but only three of these are above .300. In general, the extent of interrelationship among the rotated factors is less than that among the unrotated factors.

This is the first time there has been a notable difference between the results for the two sexes (Table XVI). Among the unrotated factors for girls there is no consistently high correlation between two factors at each age level as there was between factors II and IV for boys. Only three of the twelve significant coefficients exceed .300. The correlations among rotated factors for girls reveal a surprising fact. At each age level there is one coefficient between rotated factors which is numerically larger than any coefficient among unrotated factors. The reverse was true in the boys' data. For both boys and girls the coefficient between II and III for rotated factors is negative and notably larger in absolute value than for unrotated factors. For both sexes there are differences between age levels, although these are smaller than the differences between any one age level and the total group.

TABLE XVI

CORRELATIONS AMONG FACTORS FOR ALIEN POPULATIONS AT EACH AGE LEVEL

AGE LEVEL		UNROTATED FACTORS I	II	III	IV		ROTATED FACTORS I	II	III	IV
				BOYS ALIEN POPULATION						
Age 13	II	−.355*				II	.278*			
N = 140	III	−.372*	.219*			III	.014	−.448*		
	IV	−.208	−.485*	−.049		IV	−.300*	−.005	−.247*	
Age 14	II	−.153				II	.228*			
N = 136	III	−.216	−.038			III	.190	−.256*		
	IV	−.317*	−.424*	−.100		IV	.075	.109	−.245*	
Age 15	II	−.047				II	.014			
N = 214	III	−.052	−.163			III	.351*	−.236*		
	IV	−.200*	−.508*	−.019		IV	−.038	.155	−.139	
Age 16	II	.000				II	.164			
N = 139	III	−.105	−.037			III	.231*	−.102		
	IV	−.275*	−.414*	−.160		IV	.036	.118	−.062	
Age 17	II	−.069				II	.191			
N = 108	III	−.263*	−.036			III	.082	−.339*		
	IV	−.380*	−.446*	−.073		IV	−.016	.085	−.174	
				GIRLS ALIEN POPULATION						
Age 13	II	−.217				II	.044			
N = 120	III	−.147	−.184			III	.021	−.564*		
	IV	−.215	−.410*	−.144		IV	.020	−.034	.171	
Age 14	II	−.112				II	.287*			
N = 151	III	−.294*	−.243*			III	.201	−.401*		
	IV	−.199	−.330*	−.183		IV	.156	.106	.169	
Age 15	II	−.054				II	.190*			
N = 201	III	−.086	−.147			III	.281*	−.189*		
	IV	−.335*	−.295*	−.252*		IV	.238*	.048	.372*	
Age 16	II	−.219*				II	.191			
N = 181	III	−.190	−.056			III	.052	−.318*		
	IV	−.233*	−.119	−.280*		IV	.196*	−.158	.182	
Age 17	II	−.238*				II	.174			
N = 133	III	−.200	−.117			III	.087	−.314*		
	IV	−.224	−.218	−.239*		IV	.136	−.009	.224	

* $r\sqrt{N-1} \geqq 2.58$.

Examination of Table XVI appears to warrant the generalization that in so far as relationships among factors are concerned, one may expect considerable change in going from the total group to subgroups, and somewhat smaller but nevertheless significant changes between subgroups. The rotation of factors in this study seemed to improve the situation for boys (in the sense of relationships being closer to those of the Master Group) and to make matters worse for girls.

A Comment on Table XIV

In the preceding section, which discussed the correlations between the original variables and the general factor, it was noted that the correlation coefficients between the Clerical Speed and Accuracy test and the unrotated and rotated first factors for 13-year-old boys (Table XIV) seemed inconsistent with the corresponding coefficients at older age levels. The coefficient between the test and unrotated factor I seemed surprisingly low, and that between the test and rotated factor I was surprisingly high and negative. It was indicated then that a clue to an explanation may lie in the relationships among factors for 13-year-old boys. Table XVI shows that the numerically largest correlation coefficient between unrotated factors I and III occurs at age 13. The coefficient of correlation between the Clerical test and unrotated factor I with unrotated factor III partialled out was found to be .466. This value is in contrast to a zero-order coefficient of .135 between the Clerical test and unrotated factor I. Table XVI also discloses that rotated factors I and IV are significantly correlated ($r =$ —.300) only for age level 13. Whereas the zero-order coefficient between the Clerical test and rotated factor I was —.373, the partial coefficient with factor IV partialled out is —.247. In each instance, the partial coefficients for age 13 are more in line with the zero-order coefficients for older age levels. The inconsistency in Table XIV apparently may be explained by the interrelationships among factors at age 13 rather than by any marked differences in the relationships between the Clerical test and the general and reasoning power factors.

5

INTERPRETATION OF THE RESULTS

THE FUNDAMENTAL problem of this study has been stated earlier as "Does the general factor decrease in importance as age increases?" In order to arrive at an answer to this question a general factor was identified and studied at five age levels. The percentage of variance accounted for by the first factor at different age levels did not change much from age to age. Comparisons among the correlation coefficients between the original variables and the general factor for the different age levels, i.e., comparisons among the estimated factor loadings for the various age levels, showed relatively few significant differences. The differences that were significant indicated higher coefficients for the older age levels. These comparisons showed that the relationships between the original variables and the general factor remain substantially the same as age increases. A possible speculation as to general tendency would be that there is slight increase in relationship with increasing age. The two types of analysis yielded consistent results. There was no evidence of a decrease in importance of the general factor as age increased. The general factor seemed to maintain its importance at all the age levels, and, if anything, showed a slight tendency toward increased importance. This was true of the findings for both sexes. The answer to the question posed at the beginning of this paragraph would appear to be "No." However, an unqualified "No," although pleasantly free of ambiguity, is not a complete answer. It is necessary to consider the frame of reference in which the experiment was conducted and to determine the conditions under which the answer of "No" is accurate and complete. In a study which is based on the test results of subjects, two of the most important determiners of the results are obviously the subjects and the tests. Another determiner, no less important, is the method of analysis used. The solution to the problem of the study must be viewed in the light of these determiners in order to arrive at a scientifically meaningful conclusion.

<h2 style="text-align:center">DETERMINERS OF RESULTS</h2>

In this investigation, the subjects included children in the age range 13 to 17. It immediately follows that a condition to be placed on the final results is that they are applicable to children *in the age range considered*. Extensions of the conclusions to older and younger groups may possibly be justified on various grounds but they are not directly supported by the evidence presented in this study. In considering the subjects of the study, it is important also to note the possible effects of selection on the results. It has been indicated earlier that the subjects on which the final results are based included a representative sample of children in grades 8 through 12 of the public schools of one community not included in the Master Group (Mount Vernon, N. Y.). This sample was then classified according to age, from 13 to 17. It became evident that some of the less able 13-year-olds may have been in grade 7 or lower at the time of testing and hence were not included in the 13-year-old group. At the other extreme, some of the most able 17-year-olds may have been in college and therefore were not included in the 17-year-old group. With regard to the 13-year-olds, it was possible to estimate the percentage of children of that age who were in grade 7 or lower. This was found to be approximately 25 per cent, a sizable proportion. The percentage of 17-year-olds who were attending college was not determined. However, it is possible to estimate indirectly the proportion of 17-year-olds who had been graduated from high school before the testing program was administered. Table XI (page 44), which gives the age and grade distribution of the secondary sample, shows that for age level 16, approximately 14 per cent of the boys and 19 per cent of the girls are in grade 12. Presumably, these children will have been graduated when they are 17 years old. It is reasonable to assume that the same proportions of the present 17-year-old group were no longer in high school at the time of testing. Another factor which would tend to influence the makeup of the 17-year-old group, and to a smaller extent the 16-year-old group, is the number of children who leave school to go to work. Both of these factors are restrictive influences on the groups concerned. But the restriction tends to be at the extremes of each group. The children who are 13 years old and have not yet attained the eighth grade are, in general, the duller children. Therefore, the 13-year-old group in this study is restricted at the lower end. The exclusion of 17-year-olds who are in college means restriction of that age group at the upper end. Since children who drop out to go to work are typically at the lower end of ability, the 17-year-old group may be restricted at the lower end as well. Restriction of range is usually reflected in the size of correlation coefficients; the coefficients tend to be lower than they should be. In the correlations between the Differential Aptitude Tests and the general factor, reduced coefficients might be expected for the 13- and 17-year age levels.

Consequently, the percentage of variance accounted for by the general factor at each age level may be underestimated for age levels 13 and 17. Table XIII (page 47) shows that the percentage of variance accounted for by the general factor at age 13 is considerably lower than the corresponding figure for the older levels. It would seem more reasonable, in the light of the discussion, to consider the statistic for age 13 an underestimate, and to accept the possibility that there is no real difference between ages 13 and 14, than to claim a definite increase in the importance of the general factor between ages 13 and 14.

At the other end of the age range, at age level 17, there seems to be no indication of restriction. The correlation coefficients between the Differential Aptitude Tests and the general factor do not show any marked drop between age 15, for instance, and age 17. In fact, there are no significant differences between the coefficients for ages 15 and 17 for either sex, and six of the sixteen coefficients are higher for the older group. Similarly, the percentage of variance accounted for by the general factor at age 17 is not markedly different from the percentages at ages 14, 15, and 16. There are two possible explanations of all these facts with regard to age level 17: either there is very little restriction at the upper and lower ends of that group, or despite restrictions the correlation coefficients and percentage of variance are of the magnitude found. In either case, the evidence does not point to a decrease in the importance of the general factor as age increases but rather to no change or to an increase.

The second important determiner of the results of this study is the battery of tests used. Only one test, Clerical Speed and Accuracy, is a test given under speed conditions. The remaining seven tests are power tests. It may be expected, then, that a general factor extracted from these tests would be much more closely associated with power than with speed. Inspection of the seven power tests indicates that with the exception of the Spelling test all tests call for some type of reasoning. The completion of analogies in the Verbal Reasoning test, the understanding of numerical relationships in the Numerical Ability test, the discovery of a principle in the Abstract Reasoning test, the judgments of how objects look if constructed and rotated in the Space Relations test, the understanding of pictorially presented mechanical situations in the Mechanical Reasoning test, and even the distinction between good and bad grammar and the determination of proper usage in the Sentences test, all call for some form of reasoning ability. It would seem appropriate to consider the general factor extracted from the tests of this study as a factor heavily saturated with reasoning power, the word "reasoning" being broadly defined. This puts the factor rather close to general intelligence, which, perhaps, it is. The result is further qualification of the conclusion: the general factor does not decrease in importance (for the age range considered) *when the general factor is essentially a power factor saturated with reasoning ability.*

The methods of analyzing the data constitute the third important class of determiners of the results. The applicability of the methods to the problem, and the underlying assumptions of the methods, directly affect the outcomes of the study. In the present investigation, factor analysis was used as the means for isolating a general factor. Factor scores were then computed for the Alien Populations from regression equations. Both of these methods assume linear relationships among the variables. It is conceivable that some relationships among variables, especially when age enters into the picture, are actually curvilinear. If this is so, a linear equation does not do full justice to the extent of underlying relationship among variables. Nevertheless, all factor methods and their resulting regression equations assume linear relationships. The methods thus become easier to work with, but it must be remembered that there may be some distortion because of the simplicity.

The use of a statistical technique implies more than the application of a particular formula. The sample to which the formula is applied plays a large role in determining the final outcomes. In this study, the factor analysis to identify the general factor was made on a combination of all age levels. The reason for using a combined group was that a general factor common to all age levels could thus be extracted. The identical general factor was then studied at different age levels. However, if the factorial structure is orthogonal for the combination of age levels, there is no assurance that it will remain so at each age level. The alternative procedure is to make a separate factor analysis for each age level and then compare the general factors of the different levels. In these circumstances the factorial structure would be orthogonal for each level, but the general factors would not be the same. For the present investigation it was felt most important to keep the general factor the same at all age levels, so that comparisons among ages would be meaningful. Separate factor analyses of each age group were consequently not made. The conclusions of this study are therefore based on a general factor which was the same variable at all age levels.

The general factor has been identified as a factor very closely associated with reasoning power. As a check on this identification, the original factor structure was rotated in order to isolate a factor which could more definitely be called general reasoning power. This rotated factor was based solely on the tests which called for some kind of reasoning; the weights for Spelling, Clerical Speed and Accuracy, and Grade Placement were reduced to a minimum. The correlation coefficients between the original tests and the rotated factor of reasoning power were computed for every age level and compared with each other. The picture of changes in correlation with the rotated factor as age increased was the same as that of changes in correlation with the general factor. If change in relationship with the tests is taken as a criterion, then the general factor behaves very much like a reasoning power factor as age increases. This, together with the inspection of the loadings of the general factor, would seem to make quite reasonable the association of the general factor with reasoning power. The primary purpose of the rotations was to permit the comparison of a reasoning power factor with the general factor. A secondary purpose of the rotations will be discussed in connection with the stability of factor relationships.

The findings of this study may now be restated: *A general factor which is closely associated with reasoning ability and is primarily a power rather than a speed factor does not decrease in importance in the age range 13 to 17. There are some indications of a slight increase in importance for those years. These results hold true when the* same *general factor is studied at each age, under the assumption of linear relationships among variables. Separate analyses for boys and girls yield similar results.*

Garrett, Bryan, and Perl Study

These conclusions do not coincide with those of some other investigations in the same general area. Notable among these is the study reported in 1935 by Garrett, Bryan, and Perl [13]. This study was cited in Chapter 2. Briefly, these authors worked with 9-, 12-, and 15-year-old boys and girls. They made separate factor analyses of each age group of the same sex and found one large factor which they interpreted as "general ability to perform mental tasks of the kind presented by our tests." It was reported that the "first factor accounts for progressively less of the variance of the ten tests (except at age 12, boys) as age increases." The authors concluded that abilities of the sort measured by their tests become more specific with age. These findings seem to be inconsistent with those of the present study, and some explanation should be attempted.

When the conclusions of the present investigation were presented earlier in this chapter, it was noted that there are at least three determiners of results which have bearing on the outcomes of the study: the subjects, the tests, and the methods of analysis.

It seemed worth while to analyze the study by Garrett, Bryan, and Perl in the light of these determiners to ascertain whether some explanation may be given of the seeming disparity between the results of that study and those of the present investigation.

An obvious difference between the two studies is in the subjects. Garrett, Bryan, and Perl studied 9-, 12-, and 15-year-old children; the present investigator studied children from age 13 to age 17. If the relationship between a general factor and age is thought of as a curve, it is theoretically possible that the slope of the curve from age 9 to age 12 and from age 12 to age 15 is much steeper than the slope from age 13 or 14 to age 17. The difference in slope would account for marked changes at the earlier ages and for relative stability at the older levels. It is not unreasonable to think that a general factor may change radically at the early ages and then become stable at about the onset of adolescence.

But another issue must be considered. The type of general factor found by Garrett, Bryan, and Perl must be analyzed. This brings in the second class of determiners of results—the tests that were used. Garrett, Bryan, and Perl used ten tests four of which were classified as "non-memory" tests and six as "memory" tests. The non-memory tests were these:

Making Gates.—A simple motor speed test—2 minutes.

Vocabulary.—A sixty-item, multiple-choice test—8 minutes.

Arithmetic.—A test of forty arithmetical problems—20 minutes.

Likert-Quasha Revision of the Minnesota Paper Form Board.—A test of spatial perception—25 minutes.

The memory tests were:

Logical Prose.—Recalling a story; score is total number of ideas correctly recalled—8 minutes.

Word-Word.—A set of cards is shown with two words on each card; then a set with one of the words on the card is shown, and the second word is to be recalled—10 minutes.

Word Retention.—Two sets of words shown; recall by writing down the words—10 minutes.

Digit Span.—Remembering a sequence of digits—15 minutes.

Geometrical Forms.—A series of cards each containing a geometrical form is shown; another set containing duplicates of drawings in the first set and new drawings is then shown. Calls for recognition of forms seen before—5 minutes.

Objects.—Remembering objects seen in a display diagram; time of exposure: 30 seconds—10 minutes.

Three of the ten tests, Vocabulary, Arithmetic, and the Form Board, had time limits considered long enough to make these tests measures of power rather than of speed. Seven of the tests had speed as an important element. It would be expected, then, that a general factor (a factor common to all the tests) would be quite heavily saturated with speed of performance. Furthermore, the tests in general are of the "simple" type. They are relatively short tests and, with the possible exception of Arithmetic and the Form Board, do not call for any complex reasoning processes. Six of the tests are definitely tests of various kinds of memory. Of the remaining four, one (Making Gates) is almost purely speed and a second is a vocabulary test. A general factor derived from this battery would then be very closely associated with speed and memory. In contrast to this, the general factor of the present study is closely associated with power and reasoning.

It is clear that the general factor of Garrett, Bryan, and Perl is not the same as the general factor found by the writer. The term "general factor" can be very misleading. It is used in different studies to identify a factor common to an entire battery. If two batteries are radically different it is practically inevitable that the general factors will be different. This was recognized by Garrett, Bryan, and Perl when they identified their first factor as "general ability to perform mental tasks of the kind presented by our tests." The difference in general factors alone would go a long way toward explaining the difference in the outcomes of the Garrett, Bryan, and Perl study and the present study. However, the third important class of determiners of results, the methods of analysis, should also be examined for clues to an explanation of the disparity of results.

Garrett, Bryan, and Perl made a separate factor analysis for each age group of the same sex. The loadings of the first factor are given for each group in Table XVII, together with the reported reliability of each test for each group. Inspection of the table leads immediately to certain observations. First, the reliabilities

TABLE XVII

First Factor Loadings and Reliabilities by Age and Sex
from Garrett, Bryan, and Perl Study [13]

Test	BOYS			GIRLS		
	Age 9	Age 12	Age 15	Age 9	Age 12	Age 15
Making Gates	.392	.469	.304	.527	.332	.436
	.87*	.72	.74	.87	.58	.87
Vocabulary	.589	.656	.705	.559	.750	.623
	.84	.87	.85	.80	.89	.84
Arithmetic	.719	.781	.486	.659	.648	.602
	.88	.88	.59	.90	.84	.82
Form Board	.230	.669	.178	.513	.657	.408
	.83	.88	.86	.91	.93	.86
Logical Prose	.702	.747	.329	.730	.600	.507
	.75	.77	.46	.75	.65	.72
Word-Word	.422	.413	.282	.500	.450	.440
	.67	.54	.66	.51	.56	.63
Word Retention	.656	.447	.013	.519	.159	.321
	.56	.68	.51	.62	.62	.58
Digit Span	.341	.363	.297	.600	.286	.243
	.63	.59	.59	.55	.72	.62
Geometric Forms	.425	.369	.242	.377	.186	.289
	.78	.52	.44	.61	.31	.16
Objects	.820	.558	.230	.506	.390	.319
	.75	.59	.52	.66	.52	.55
Percentage of Variance	31	32	12	31	24	19
N	108	96	102	117	100	123

* Reliability coefficients are shown below the factor loadings.

of the original tests for some of the groups are extremely low. Eleven of the thirty reported reliability coefficients for boys are below .60; six of the eleven are for 15-year-olds. For girls, there are nine reliability coefficients below .60. A second observation is that the percentage of variance accounted for by the first factor decreases sharply between ages 12 and 15 for boys but shows a considerably smaller decrease between those ages for girls. In general, the test reliabilities for 15-year-old girls are higher than the reliabilities for 15-year-old boys. The percentage of variance for a given age is based on the factor loadings for that age. These factor loadings, in turn, are estimated coefficients of correlation between the tests and the factor. Low reliability for the tests usually causes attenuation of the correlation coefficients and would result in a smaller percentage of variance. Perhaps, then, the sharp drop in percentage of variance between 12- and 15-year-old boys and the much smaller drop for girls is explained by the lower reliabilities of the tests for 15-year-old boys.

A third and very important observation is that the general factor at each age level is not the *same* variable. The results are based on separate factor analyses. Although the first factors of the different groups may be similar, they are not the same. The percentage of variance accounted for is given for *each* general factor. So long as these statistics are taken as indications of the characteristics of general factors at different age levels no confusion arises. But if comparisons are made between the general factor at one age and the general factor at another age, it must be remembered that the same variable is not being studied.

Purely as a matter of theoretical interest, the writer made the assumption that the study by Garrett, Bryan, and Perl had the same general factor at each age level. Under this assumption the factor loadings at each age represent correlation coefficients between the original tests and the same general factor. As correlation coefficients, the different age loadings for a given test may be compared. The loadings were therefore converted to z-functions and the difference between z's was divided by the standard error of the difference to get an estimate of the significance of the difference between any two loadings. The results are given in Table XVIII. A value of 2.58 or higher for the ratio of the difference between z's to the standard error of the difference indicates a difference significant at the 1 per cent level. This has been taken as indicative of a real difference. It will be seen that for boys there are a total of eleven significant differences out of a possible thirty. Ten of these differences indicate that the correlation coefficient is lower for the older group. The significant differences appear in the loadings for the following tests: Arithmetic, Form Board, Logical Prose, Word Retention, and Objects. Nine of the eleven significant differences are with age 15. For all the tests concerned except the Form Board, the reliability for age 15 is below .60. For the Form Board the reliability is high for all age levels, but the loading for age 12 looks like an artifact. It is .669 compared to .230 and .178 for ages 9 and 15, respectively. For girls, there are only five differences significant at the 1 per cent level, and these

TABLE XVIII

FACTOR LOADINGS OF GARRETT, BRYAN, AND PERL STUDY TREATED AS CORRELATION COEFFICIENTS, AND SIGNIFICANCE OF DIFFERENCES

Test	Age	BOYS				GIRLS			
		Loading	Ratio of Difference to Standard Error* Age 9	Age 12	Test Reliability	Loading	Ratio of Difference to Standard Error* Age 9	Age 12	Test Reliability
Making Gates	9	.392	.67		.87	.527	-1.75		.87
	12	.469	-.72	-1.35	.72	.332	-.91	.89	.58
	15	.304			.74	.436			.87
Vocabulary	9	.589	.77		.84	.559	2.48		.80
	12	.656	1.44	.63	.87	.750	.75	-1.77	.89
	15	.705			.85	.623			.84
Arithmetic	9	.719	1.00		.88	.659	-.14		.90
	12	.781	-2.68	-3.59	.88	.648	-.72	-.55	.84
	15	.486			.59	.602			.82
Form Board	9	.230	4.05		.83	.513	1.60		.91
	12	.669	-.39	-4.37	.88	.657	-1.02	-2.59	.93
	15	.178			.86	.408			.86
Logical Prose	9	.702	.67		.75	.730	-1.71		.75
	12	.747	-3.78	-4.34	.77	.600	-2.82	-.98	.65
	15	.329			.46	.507			.72
Word-Word	9	.422	-.08		.67	.500	-.47		.51
	12	.413	-1.14	-1.04	.54	.450	-.59	-.09	.56
	15	.282			.66	.440			.63
Word Retention	9	.656	-2.15		.56	.519	-3.00		.62
	12	.447	-5.52	-3.25	.68	.159	-1.85	1.26	.62
	15	.013			.51	.321			.58
Digit Span	9	.341	.18		.63	.600	-2.89		.55
	12	.363	-.35	-.51	.59	.286	-3.40	-.34	.72
	15	.297			.59	.243			.62
Geometric Forms	9	.425	-.47		.78	.377	-1.51		.61
	12	.369	-1.48	-.97	.52	.186	-.76	.80	.31
	15	.242			.44	.289			.16
Objects	9	.820	-3.71		.75	.506	-1.05		.66
	12	.558	-6.59	-2.75	.59	.390	-1.73	-.59	.52
	15	.230			.52	.319			.55

* Values of 2.58 or higher indicate significance at 1% level or less. Negative differences indicate higher coefficients for younger groups.

indicate lower loadings for the older groups. Here the reliabilities do not seem to be so much at fault, but the loadings for Word Retention (.519, .159, .321) and for Digit Span (.600, .286, .243) are somewhat inconsistent from age to age. The purpose of this analysis is to indicate that a portion of the large drop in the percentage of variance accounted for by the first factor, for boys between 12 and 15, is probably due to unreliability of the tests. Perhaps if the reliability coefficients for 15-year-old boys had been higher, the drop of 20 percentage points between ages 12 and 15 would have come closer to the 5 per cent drop for girls. It cannot be denied that, as the data stand, the tendency seems to be toward decrease in the importance of the general factor. But the extent of decrease is difficult to evaluate. The writer wishes to repeat that this last analysis was made under a hypothetical assumption. If it is accepted at all, it indicates what has been briefly stated earlier: the low reliability coefficients for some groups may have accentuated the size of differences and tended to overemphasize the decrease in percentage of variance as age increased.

The significant outcome of the writer's analysis of the Garrett, Bryan, and Perl study is not that the decreasing importance of the general factor may be exaggerated but rather that it clearly points out the conditions and qualifications which must be placed on studies of a general factor. In part this was very aptly stated by Asch [3] when he wrote, "Authors of theories of mental organization should be expected to state the age range over which their theories are valid." In addition to defining the subjects it is essential to define as clearly as possible just what is being investigated. In the present study it was the general factor which needed definition, and the definition provided includes an indication of how the general factor was obtained and studied. It seems to the writer that much of the lack of understanding of the results of studies in this general area and much of the disagreement between studies is basically a question of semantics. If the key words and qualifiers were clearly defined, many difficulties would dissolve.

IMPLICATIONS

An implication of the present study and, indeed, of all studies, is the importance of clear-cut explanations of the key words and of the qualifications which must be placed on the conclusions. The comparisons between the present findings and those of Garrett, Bryan, and Perl emphasize this implication. Unless such explanations are available the results of different studies in the same area become confused by semantic difficulties. Specifically, in the area of the present investigation, a term such as "general factor" must be explained in terms of the tests and subjects from which it was derived and the manner in which it was studied. These explanations serve not only to clarify the findings but to indicate the conditions which must be placed on the results.

The importance of clear-cut explanations is quite obvious and, as has been said, applies to all studies. In fact, most investigators indicate, in the statement of their conclusions, the conditions under which their results were obtained and the limitations of their findings. But there is a real danger when several different studies are examined and an over-all deduction is made. Because of the lack of uniformity in the meaning of terms used in factorial studies, a general factor derived from a battery of simple speed tests and a general factor derived from a battery of complex power tests eventually come to be taken as the same general factor or *the* general factor. Not infrequently it is called *g*, the general underlying ability of Spearman. However, it must be recalled that Spearman [20] explained that one must use an absolutely *random* set of tests to find the real *g*, for any deviation from randomness will bias the nature of the general factor found. This bias frequently accounts for contradictory results in studies each of which has investigated a general factor. Nevertheless, studies which work with various types of general factor do contribute to a greater understanding of a complex phenomenon. Each is actually exploring a limited aspect of the area of relationships among abilities, and so long as the particular bias is recognized and understood, the study permits of greater understanding of the area.

A second implication of the present investigation stems directly from the study of the general factor at five different age levels. This study suggests that the underlying general ability of an individual does not decrease as he grows older but rather is maintained and even tends to increase. The increase apparently is small in the range of years considered in this study but there certainly is no evidence of decrease. This statement is predicated on the definition of general factor as given in this investigation, i.e., a general factor closely associated with reasoning ability and with power rather than speed. The general factor found by Garrett, Bryan, and Perl cannot be defined in the same way, and it should be no surprise that the findings of those authors are different from the findings of this writer. The general intellective bi-factor studied by Swineford [21] comes closer to the definition given above, and her findings are confirmed by the present study. She reported: "No evidence is found to support the view that with increasing mental maturity the general factor plays a less important role as special abilities are developed. On the contrary, the general ability represented in the present data increases in both its absolute and its relative contribution to the total test variance." In the study on which the quotation is based, Swineford retested the same cases after an interval of time. In a later cross-section study in which she tested children in grades 5 to 10, Swineford [22] confirmed her earlier statements, and her conclusions with regard to the general bi-factor are notable: "On the basis of the foregoing evidence, the general bi-factor defined by the present battery of nine tests may be described with confidence as general mental ability, for it exhibits the characteristics of general mental ability. It is positively correlated with mental tests and with school achievement. It increases with chronological age during the period represented by Grades V–X. It is possessed in greater amount by normal pupils than by dull pupils, where brightness is defined by grade placement. There are no statistically significant sex differences."

A point of view which would reconcile the findings of various studies is that the general factor of any investigation is actually a composite made up of reasoning ability, speed, memory, perception, rote skills, and other abilities. With increasing maturity various components such as, perhaps, rote skills and memory detach themselves from the general mass and may be identified as distinct abilities or factors. The underlying general reasoning ability tends to remain, however, along with varying amounts of the other components. A factor analysis of a wide-range age group tested with a battery that tends to favor reasoning ability would of necessity yield a general factor which is principally the relatively stable reasoning ability. Other components are still present as indicated by the loadings of non-reasoning tests, but these components are now relatively minor. The use of a heterogeneous age sample would tend to eliminate what is not common to all ages. Whereas motor skill, for example, may fall into the general factor for a particular age group, it may become more specific at an older level. In this hypothetical situation the general factor of the younger age group might appear to be more important than the one at the older level, while the reasoning ability component of the general factor remained substantially the same. If the tests used in the analysis are principally reasoning tests, the reasoning ability component of the general factor—the stable component—may be expected to be even more pronounced. Reasoning ability itself is not a well-defined single entity. It is probably a conglomerate of various kinds of reasoning ability, each of which is used in a different situation. If a single word were desired to express the connotations of general reasoning ability, probably the best choice would be "intelligence." Under ordinary conditions, the basic intelligence or power of an individual does not deteriorate until the person is well advanced in years. Over a short span of years, during adolescence and early adulthood, it may remain at a relatively constant level; over longer periods of time it may increase, but seldom does it decrease.

An interesting implication with regard to differentiation of abilities may be deduced from the findings of this study. If the general factor accounts for approximately the same percentage of variance of the scores at each age level (assuming the data given for age 13 are underestimates), then it would appear that there is no greater differentiation at age 17 than at age 13 or 14. That is to say, the differentiation of abilities, which is fundamentally a progressive reduction of the general factor in favor of specialization, is as marked at the beginning of the secondary school years as it is at the end of those years. It must be noted that this is true when the general factor is closely associated with underlying reasoning power. It is to be expected that such a factor would be extracted from tests that are, for the most part, tests of various kinds of reasoning ability. There is no evidence that a general factor extracted from simple motor speed tests, for example, would exhibit the kind of stability over a range of years that was noted for the general factor of this study. Viewed in another light, the progressive reduction of the general factor which occurs with some tests may actually be the breaking away of various components until the core of reasoning ability is left. The differentiation is, then, in a sense, dependent upon conditions of testing. Under some conditions, it may be possible to determine the organization of abilities which will be maintained for the next five years or longer. If desired, separate measures of speed, rote skills, perceptual ability, and the like might be obtained without affecting the basic pattern of relationships among certain abilities.

To a counselor there is a decided advantage in dealing with measures which exhibit the same interrelationships over a period of years. Comparison of groups or of successive testings of the same individual becomes more meaningful. The differences in scores may be examined without the feeling that the interrelationships among abilities have changed to the extent of altering the meaning of the measures. A note of caution must be inserted here. A test score is, in the last analysis, a determination of the number of right answers to a series of questions. Different processes will be used by different students to arrive at the answers. Nothing in the test scores or in any statistical manipulation of them reveals the mental processes that were used. It is therefore impossible to say that a test is identically the same for two groups of individuals or even for two people. A counselor must be aware of the fact that there are various processes for determining the right answer to a question although there is little he can do with such information. This clouding of the meaning of test scores is, at this time, irremediable. But the added confusion which comes from changing interrelationships among abilities, and the consequent changes in meaning of scores, may perhaps be eliminated. A series of tests which exhibits a stable pattern of interrelationships at least minimizes this additional source of confusion.

THE STABILITY OF FACTOR RELATIONSHIPS

The most significant conclusion that may be drawn from the analysis of the relationships among factors is that the population plays a very important role in determining the factor structure. That there are two major variables which determine factorial structure—the tests and the population—would be readily admitted. But very often it seems that the role played by the subjects or population is either underestimated or forgotten. Factors are derived from the analysis of intertest correlation coefficients for a given population. New tests are sometimes made on the basis of the factors and an examination of the content of the original test variables. These new tests are then presumably relatively pure measures of various factors and are administered to populations quite different from the original subjects. The scores are taken as indications of standing or ability in the different factors. It is always remembered that the factor is determined by the content of the test; it is not always remembered that the factor is also determined by the subjects who take the test.

In the present study a set of orthogonal factors was derived from a wide-range age sample—the Master Group. These factors were statistically independent of each other. A check with a wide-range age sample drawn from the Alien Population yielded results compatible with the supposition of independent factors. But when the different age levels of the Alien Population were studied separately, there were notable changes in the interrelationships among factors. Unrotated factors II and IV, which exhibited a negligible relationship ($r = -.152$) for a combined-age sample, were correlated at each age level. The coefficients ranged from $-.414$ to $-.508$. This change in relationship between the two factors is probably due to the effect of age. In the combined-age sample, age is a variable which influences the interrelationships among the factors. In a single age level, the variable of age is controlled; in effect, it is partialed out. A relatively strong relationship which exists between the two factors when age is controlled tends to be obliterated in the combined sample where age is an active variable. The independent factors of the wide-range age group thus are related factors when a portion of that very group is studied. The implication is obviously that the factor structure for a single age group is not the same as that for a combined age group, under the condition of relative independence of factors. Inspection of Table XVI reveals that not only are the relationships among unrotated factors noticeably different between a combined age sample and single age groups, but there are also differences from age group to age group. The differences are not large —there is no complete change of factor pattern in going from one age level to another or even from the Master Group to a single age level. After all, the tests are the same and the children differ primarily only in age, and in that by no more than a few years. But if, even under such conditions, the differences in relationships among factors are sufficiently marked to indicate that the factors differ from one group to another, then such a thing as a "pure factor test" is ambiguous. The very factor which is being "purely measured" may not exist in that form at all when the population is changed. Jeffress [16] examined the problem of variation of "primary abilities" from one population to another. He set up a hypothetical problem with two populations. One was assumed to have two primary abilities; the second was assumed to have three primary abilities. He reconstructed the correlation coefficients for each group, combined the two, and made a factor analysis of the combination. The result was five factors, two of which were not obviously related to anything in the original tables of factors. Jeffress makes the point that if groups require different factors to account for the variance then it is likely that some individuals will require more factors and other individuals will require fewer factors for adequate explanation. "Only by the analysis of results from a great variety of samples can we hope to determine the extent to which the 'primary abilities' will vary from one population to another, and even then the variation from person to person within the sample must remain a troublesome possibility." The data of the present study tend to bear out Jeffress' conclusion. In so far as unrotated factors are concerned, it would seem that somewhat different factors appear as the group changes even slightly. If it is desired to isolate primary abilities, then it is also necessary to consider carefully the points made by Jeffress.

That changes in the group may result in changes in factorial composition of the same tests is further confirmed by Balinsky [4]. He gave the Wechsler-Bellevue Intelligence Scale to various age samplings between ages 9 and 60. The respective age samplings were 9 years, 12 years, 15 years, 25–29 years, 35–44 years, and

50–59 years. For each age level he obtained the intercorrelations among the subtests of the scale and made a factor analysis. Among his conclusions Balinsky wrote: "As a result of the above findings it could be stated that the mental traits change and undergo reorganization over a span of years. Therefore, when interpreting tests of intelligence, it is of importance to take into consideration the age of the individual. The same test, given to a person of a certain age, may not be measuring the same abilities in him that it would measure when given to an older or younger person. Even though the whole intelligence scale may yield the same factors for a wide span of years, the separate tests that compose the scale may not necessarily be described in terms of the same factors from age to age."

In the present investigation the writer had to decide between a study of a general factor which was the same variable throughout the age range 13 to 17 or a study of five different general factors. The former course was decided upon because it was felt that in that way a study could be made of a factor which was general, in the sense of running through all the variables, and also the same for each age level. In order to obtain such a general factor it was necessary to use a population made up of all age levels. It was recognized, however, that the clarity of comparisons gained by using the same general factor at all age levels would be offset by a confusion in the relationships among the general factor and other factors when each age level was considered separately. The data confirm the belief that if the condition of orthogonality of factors is to be maintained at each age level and for a combined group of all age levels, then a separate factor analysis should be made for each group, resulting in factors that differ from group to group.

The primary reason for computing the correlation coefficients among the rotated factors was to determine whether there is a change in the degree of stability of a factor pattern after rotations have been made. It must be noted that the principal purpose of rotations is to arrive at psychologically more meaningful factors than those presented in the unrotated pattern. To achieve this end it is necessary to have at least several measures of the same ability so that identification may be made. The present study is limited in this respect. There is, for example, only one test of numerical ability. It would be impossible, therefore, to identify a numerical group factor in any factorial analysis. Indeed, other than the one rotated factor which may be considered a general reasoning power factor, no attempt has been made to name the remaining rotated factors. It cannot then be maintained that the effect of rotations on the stability of factors is being put to a crucial test in this investigation. However, names could have been assigned to each of the rotated factors, perhaps even with a certain amount of justification. Inspection of the rotated factor loadings will reveal this to be so. The problem which is to be considered here is: Do rotations which seem to produce a more or less meaningful pattern, and which might result in plausible names for factors, produce a more stable structure than the unrotated factors?

The data of Table XVI show that, in general, there is no greater stability in the relationships among the rotated factors of the Master Group when they are applied to single age levels than there is in the relationships among the unrotated factors. For boys, the relationships among the unrotated factors seem to have been "spread out" among the rotated factors. The coefficients among rotated factors tend to be lower than the coefficients among unrotated factors although there is the same number of significant relationships. But for the girls there seems to have been a concentration of relationship; at each age level there is a coefficient between rotated factors which is numerically greater than the highest coefficient among unrotated factors. Both sexes exhibit differences between age levels. With regard to the relationships among factors, the rotations did not produce a pattern notably more stable than the unrotated factors. The tendency to distribute the extent of relationship among all the factors, observed in the data for boys, is not present in the data for girls. It will be recalled that the rotations of factors for girls were not the same as those for boys. The end products, the rotated factors, were quite similar for both sexes but the actual rotations were different. Possibly the difference in rotations accounts to some extent for the spreading of relationship among the factors for boys and for the concentration of relationship between two factors for girls. The essential point is that the process of rotating factors does not in and of itself assure greater stability of interfactor relationships than that which would be obtained from unrotated factors.

Again it must be pointed out that other studies may have data more suitable for rotations and meaningful interpretation of rotated factors. It may be that in such circumstances factor interrelationships will tend to remain stable for a number of groups. In this study, the differences in relationships among factors, although real, are not very large. Perhaps these differences would not have been present had the rotated factors been clearly defined psychological entities. But it is well to recognize that stability of relationships between factors is not assured by a statistical method. It must be demonstrated for different groups of subjects and for different factors.

6

SUMMARY AND CONCLUSIONS

THE PRINCIPAL problem of this study was a test of the hypothesis that the general factor tends to decrease in importance as age increases. A secondary problem was the investigation of factor interrelationships at different age levels. The subjects, materials, and general procedure are summarized below.

Subjects.—Boys and girls in the age range 13 through 17, inclusive, tested at twenty-four school systems with the Differential Aptitude Tests.

Materials.—The Differential Aptitude Tests, a battery of eight tests constructed to measure achievement in different areas for the purposes of guidance. Seven of these tests are power tests and six of the seven call for some kind of reasoning ability.

Procedure.—From twenty-three of the school systems tested, a Master Group of 1000 cases was selected at random for boys and for girls. Each Master Group included 200 cases drawn from five age levels from 13 to 17. A factor analysis by Hotelling's method of principal components was made of the eight Differential Aptitude Tests and the grade in which the student was registered. The separate analyses for the two sexes resulted in a general factor and three additional factors, all orthogonal to each other, accounting, in each sex, for 81 per cent of the variance of the scores. Each set of factors was rotated to obtain a new set of orthogonal factors, one of which could be identified as general reasoning power. Regression equations were constructed for the purpose of estimating factor scores on each of the four unrotated and rotated factors. The equations were used to compute factor scores for all of the subjects of an Alien Population. This population was taken from the school system of Mount Vernon, New York, a system not included among those from which the Master Groups were selected. Paralleling the two Master Groups, there was an Alien Population for each sex, a total of 737 boys and 786 girls.

The general factor was studied by computing for each age level of the two Alien Populations the percentage of variance accounted for by the general factor, and the correlation coefficients between the original variables and the general factor. The secondary problem of interfactor relationships was studied by computing the intercorrelations among unrotated and rotated factors at each age level from thirteen to seventeen.

Results

The analyses indicated that the percentage of variance accounted for by the general factor was substantially the same at all age levels, and the correlation coefficients between the general factor and the original variables (the estimated general factor loadings) showed very few significant changes from age level to age level. Among the changes that were significant were higher correlation coefficients for the older age levels. As age increased, the rotated factor identified as reasoning power behaved very much like the general factor with regard to changes in correlation with the original variables. The results for both sexes were similar.

The analysis of interfactor relationships showed that the four orthogonal factors of the Master Groups did not remain orthogonal at each age level of the Alien Populations. There were marked differences in some interfactor relationships between the Master Group and single age levels and smaller differences between age levels. No greater stability of relationships was achieved by the rotations of factors made in this study.

Conclusions

The general factor tends to maintain, rather than to lose, its importance as age increases. This is true under the following conditions:

1. For students in the age range considered in this study, viz., 13 through 17.

2. For a general factor which is the same statistical variable at each age level studied.

3. For a general factor which is derived from tests of reasoning ability, under power rather than speed conditions.

It is conceivable that with tests administered under speed conditions a certain amount of breakdown of the general factor may be due to the differential effects of speed of performance at different age levels. An important implication of the results is the necessity for defining a general factor in terms of the tests used, the subjects of the study, and the methods of analysis.

Throughout this study the word "reasoning" has been used liberally. The unrotated first factor, the general factor, has been associated with reasoning power; the rotated first factor has been considered a relatively purer measure of reasoning power. Neither the unrotated nor the rotated first factor is considered to be *the* reasoning factor or even a particular type of reasoning factor. No such implication of psychological unity is intended for either factor. The word "reasoning" is used here to describe factors derived from tests in which different kinds of reasoning ability are required, and it is therefore closer to general intellectual power than to a particular unitary form of reasoning.

The study of factor interrelationships indicated the great importance of the subjects in the determination of factors. Apparently, factor interrelationships change with changes in the subjects, indicating that the best factorial description of one group is not the best for another group. If a factorial test is constructed to give a measure of a certain factor, it must first be demonstrated that the factor exists in the same form in the various populations to be tested.

The rotations of factors performed in this study did not make for greater stability of factors. However, the data were severely limited with respect to an investigation of the effects of rotations. It is entirely possible that with more suitable data rotations would yield stable factors. But the results of this study suggest that rotations as such are not enough to assure stability. Stability must be demonstrated with particular factors for different groups.

BIBLIOGRAPHY

1. ANASTASI, A. *A group factor in immediate memory.* Archives of Psychology, No. 120. New York: Columbia University, 1930.
2. ANASTASI, A. *Further studies on the memory factor.* Archives of Psychology, No. 142. New York: Columbia University, 1932.
3. ASCH, S. E. *A study of change in mental organization.* Archives of Psychology, No. 195. New York: Columbia University, 1936.
4. BALINSKY, B. "An analysis of the mental factors of various age groups from nine to sixty." *Genetic Psychology Monographs,* 23: 191–234, 1941.
5. BLUMENFELD, W. "The invariability of certain coefficients of correlation during human development." *Journal of Genetic Psychology,* 68:189–204, 1946.
6. BRYAN, A. I. *Organization of memory in young children.* Archives of Psychology, No. 162. New York: Columbia University, 1934.
7. CLARK, M. P. *Changes in primary mental abilities with age.* Archives of Psychology, No. 291. New York: Columbia University, 1944.
8. *Differential Aptitude Tests Manual.* New York: The Psychological Corporation, 1947.
9. FISHER, R. A. *Statistical methods for research workers.* Edinburgh: Oliver and Boyd, 1946.
10. GARRETT, H. E. "A study of the CAVD intelligence examination." *Journal of Educational Research,* 21:103–108, 1930.
11. GARRETT, H. E. "Differentiable mental traits." *Psychological Record,* 2:259–298, 1938.
12. GARRETT, H. E. "A developmental theory of intelligence." *American Psychologist,* 1:372–378, 1946.
13. GARRETT, H. E., BRYAN, A. I., and PERL, R. E. *The age factor in mental organization.* Archives of Psychology, No. 176. New York: Columbia University, 1935.
14. HOLZINGER, K. J. and HARMAN, H. H. *Factor analysis, a synthesis of factorial methods.* Chicago: The University of Chicago Press, 1941.
15. HOTELLING, H. "Analysis of a complex of statistical variables into principal components." *Journal of Educational Psychology,* 24: 417–441, 498–520, 1933.

16. JEFFRESS, L. A. "The nature of 'primary abilities.'" *American Journal of Psychology*, 61:107–111, 1948.
17. REICHARD, S. K. *Mental organization and age level.* Archives of Psychology, No. 295. New York: Columbia University, 1944.
18. SCHILLER, B. *Verbal, numerical, and spatial abilities of young children.* Archives of Psychology, No. 161. New York: Columbia University, 1934.
19. SCHNECK, M. R. *The measurement of verbal and numerical abilities.* Archives of Psychology, No. 107. New York: Columbia University, 1929.
20. SPEARMAN, C. "Our need of some science in place of the word 'intelligence.'" *Journal of Educational Psychology*, 22:401–410, 1931.
21. SWINEFORD, F. "Growth in the general and verbal bi-factors from grade VII to grade IX." *Journal of Educational Psychology*, 38: 257–272, 1947.
22. SWINEFORD, F. *A study in factor analysis: the nature of the general, verbal, and spatial bi-factors.* Supplementary Educational Monographs, No. 67. Chicago: The University of Chicago Press, 1948.
23. THORNDIKE, E. L. *The measurement of intelligence.* New York: Bureau of Publications, Teachers College, Columbia University, 1926.
24. THURSTONE, L. L. *Primary mental abilities.* Psychometric Monographs, No. 1. Chicago: The University of Chicago Press, 1938.
25. THURSTONE, L. L. *The selection of talent.* Chicago: Psychometric Laboratory, University of Chicago, 1946, No. 30.
26. THURSTONE, L. L. and THURSTONE, T. G. *Factorial studies of intelligence.* Psychometric Monographs, No. 2. Chicago: The University of Chicago Press, 1941.
27. TUCKER, L. R. "A method for finding the inverse of a matrix." *Psychometrika*, 3:189–197, 1938.
28. War Manpower Commission, Division of Occupational Analysis. "Factor analysis of occupational aptitude tests." *Educational and Psychological Measurement*, 5:147–155, 1945.
29. WOLFLE, D. *Factor analysis to 1940.* Psychometric Monographs, No. 3. Chicago: The University of Chicago Press, 1940.

APPENDIX

THE working equation given on page 42 for estimating the rotated factor scores may be derived in the following manner [14]:

In matrix form, a factor pattern may be written:

$$(1) \qquad X = MF,$$

where X represents the variables; M, the complete pattern matrix. If A is taken to represent the matrix of coefficients of common factors and U, the diagonal matrix of unique-factor coefficients, then $M = \|AU\|$ and (1) becomes

$$(2) \qquad X = (AU)F.$$

The regression equation for predicting a common factor score, f_t, may be written:

$$(3) \qquad f_t = {}_tb_1x_1 + {}_tb_2x_2 + \cdots + {}_tb_mx_m.$$

The normal equations for the determination of the b's:

$$(4) \quad \begin{cases} b_1 + r_{12}b_2 + \cdots + b_nr_{1n} = t_{1s} \\ r_{12}b_1 + \phantom{r_{12}}b_2 + \cdots + b_nr_{2n} = t_{2s} \\ \phantom{r_{12}b_1}\vdots \\ \phantom{r_{12}b_1}\vdots \\ r_{1n}b_1 + r_{2n}b_2 + \cdots + \phantom{r_{12}}b_n = t_{ns} \end{cases}$$

The solution of equations (4) may be obtained by determinants:

$$\text{If } D = \begin{Vmatrix} 1 & t_{1s} & t_{2s} & \cdots & t_{ns} \\ t_{1s} & 1 & r_{12} & \cdots & r_{1n} \\ \vdots & & & & \\ \vdots & & & & \\ \vdots & & & & \\ t_{ns} & r_{n1} & r_{n2} & \cdots & 1 \end{Vmatrix}$$

then

$$(5) \quad b_{sj} = -\frac{D_{js}}{D_{ss}},$$

where D_{ss} is the minor of the first element (which is R, the determinant of observed correlations) and D_{js} is the cofactor of t_{js} in D (which may be expressed in terms of cofactors of R).

$$(6) \qquad .. \quad b_{sj} = \frac{1}{R}\left[t_{1s}R_{1j} + t_{2s}R_{2j} + \cdots + t_{ns}R_{nj}\right],$$

where R_{kj} is the cofactor of r_{kj} in R.

(7) $f = t'_s R^{-1} X$, where t'_s is the column vector taken from column s of the factor structure S.

In matrix form:

$$(8) \qquad\qquad F = T'R^{-1}X.$$

When the factors are uncorrelated the pattern and structure coincide and (8) becomes

$$(9) \qquad\qquad F = M'R^{-1}X.$$

To estimate a factor score, the transpose of factor loadings becomes a row vector; this row vector is postmultiplied by the inverse of the original correlation matrix and the result is multiplied by the test scores, X.